STANDING STONES

Kenneth McNally
STANDING
STONES

and other monuments of early Ireland

Appletree Press

First published and printed by
The Appletree Press Ltd
7 James Street South
Belfast BT2 8DL

First published in paperback 1988

9 8 7 6 5 4 3 2 1

British Library Cataloguing in Publication Data
McNally, Kenneth
    Standing stones and other monuments of
    early Ireland
    1. Man, Prehistoric – Ireland   2. Ireland –
    Antiquities   3. Ireland – Description and
    travel – 1981- – Guide-books
    I. Title
    914.15′04824   DA920

ISBN 0-86281-201-2

Contents

List of Photographs   7

Preface   9

1. The Tomb Builders   11

2. Stone Circles and Standing Stones   43

3. The Celtic Legacy   69

4. The Early Monasteries   91

Bibliography   127

Photographs

Kilclooney More, County Donegal	*page* 19	The Lios, County Limerick	63
Carrowmore, County Sligo	20–1	Ballynoe, County Down	64
Goward, County Down	22	The Giant's Ring, County Down	65
Knockeen, County Waterford	23	Drombeg, County Cork	66
Magheraghanrush, County Sligo	24–5	The Piper's Stones, County Wicklow	67
Proleek, County Louth	26	Reanascreena, County Cork	68
Legananny, County Down	27	Dunbeg, County Kerry	77
Tawnatruffaun, County Sligo	28	Tullaghoge, County Tyrone	78–9
Creevykeel, County Sligo	28	Cahermacnaghten, County Clare	80
Aughnacliff, County Longford	29	Lough-na-Crannagh, County Antrim	81
Woodtown, County Dublin	30	Staigue, County Kerry	82–3
Kiltiernan, County Dublin	31	Ballykinvarga, County Clare	84
Carrickglass, County Sligo	32	Caldragh Idol, County Fermanagh	85
Srahwee, County Mayo	33	Dunloe, County Kerry	86
Poulnabrone, County Clare	34	Turoe, County Galway	87
Gortnavern, County Donegal	35	Dubh Cathair, County Galway	88–9
Kilmogue, County Kilkenny	36	Grainan of Aileach, County Donegal	90
Newgrange, County Meath	37	Inishmurray, County Sligo	99
Gaulstown, County Waterford	38	Glendalough, County Wicklow	100
Cloghanmore, County Donegal	39	Moone, County Wicklow	101, 102–3
Haroldstown, County Carlow	40–1	Kilmalkedar, County Kerry	104–5, 106, 107
Coagh, County Londonderry	42	Skellig Michael, County Kerry	109
Doagh, County Antrim	52	Gallarus, County Kerry	110–11
Ardmore, County Donegal	53	Drumcliff, County Sligo	112, 113
Killadangan, County Mayo	54	Arboe, County Tyrone	114–5
Punchestown, County Kildare	55	Reask, County Kerry	116
Bocan, County Donegal	56–7	Dalkey Island, County Dublin	118
Longstone Rath, County Kildare	58	Temple Benan, County Galway	119
Bohonagh, County Cork	59	Clonfert, County Galway	120
Beaghmore, County Tyrone	60	Glencolumbkille, County Donegal	122
Beltany Tops, County Donegal	61	Monasterboice, County Louth	123, 124–5
Eightercua, County Kerry	62	Dysert O Dea, County Clare	126

Preface

The Irish countryside is rich in reminders of the past. Though the stereotyped image of Ireland abroad as a land of Round Towers and High Crosses prevails, those venerable and romanticised symbols of the island of saints and scholars tell only part of the story. For several thousand years successive groups of immigrants left tangible and often spectacular legacies of their different cultures: megalithic chamber tombs of Stone Age farmers, mysterious Bronze Age circles and standing stones, pagan gods and sanctuaries, Celtic raths and cashels, and the lonely ruins of Early Christian monasteries. Mellowed by time and weather, these ubiquitous monuments contribute to, and reflect, the personality of the landscape and the legends and folklore of its inhabitants.

Ireland's field monuments are often arrestingly visual. Even a simple standing stone, boldly faceted and encrusted with lichen, can possess an almost sculptural quality; while many of the early cross-inscribed pillars are gems of exquisite design and workmanship. Some of the most remarkable architecture of prehistory is found in the great stone tombs, particularly the tall portal-dolmens with their dramatically poised capstones weighing many tons; looming up as monstrous forms on the skyline, these astonishing structures can scarcely fail to impress even the casual observer.

Many of the monuments described in this book can be easily reached. Some are situated quite literally by the roadside, at the end of a lane or a short walk across a field or two. Others are more difficult of access and must be searched out in peat bogs, on mountain-sides and cliff-tops and remote offshore islands. A good map is essential. The Ordnance Survey half-inch series comprises 25 individual sheets each corresponding to an area of roughly county size. These maps mark many though by no means all of the better known monuments; in addition they provide the motorist with a good idea of the approach to a site as minor roads and even some footpaths are shown, together with hill contours and other physical features. Also available from the Ordnance Survey Office in Dublin is the compendious *Map of Monastic Ireland* (1964 edition): drawn to a scale of 9.86 miles to 1 inch, it records all known monastic sites, distinguishing between Celtic establishments and those of the later continental orders. Two large scale maps of regional interest are T.D. Robinson's *The Burren* and *Oilean Arann*, covering the antiquities of north-west Clare and the Aran Islands in considerable detail.

Those intent on seeking out unmarked sites in rough country will do well to carry field-glasses: a ruined megalithic tomb on a rock-strewn hill-side can be a surprisingly elusive object to the naked eye even when its approximate location is known. Neglected antiquities soon become overgrown with gorse and bracken and are especially difficult to spot. Exploring off the beaten tourist track calls for strong footwear and a certain amount of caution; some cliff-forts, for example, are extremely dangerous.

A large number of monuments in State Care are of course signposted, the name being displayed in green letters on a white background, usually in both Irish and English in the Republic, along with the official identifying number of the site. Even so, signposting tends to be erratic, and the precise whereabouts of some antiquities will only be discovered through personal enquiry in the area. When asking directions it is best to use the local name of the monument in question, if known. One of the pleasures of wandering off in search of ancient remains in the Irish countryside is the absence of restrictions. However, the fact that a monument is signposted does not always imply a right of way. Access to many sites lies across private property and where this is obvious the permission of the owner should be obtained. Very occasionally one may be required to pay a small fee 'for trespass'; but by and large, Irish farmers are remarkably tolerant of visitors on their land and will go out of their way to be helpful.

For information on all ancient monuments in State Care, and many others which are not, the reader is referred to the several comprehensive guidebooks listed in the Bibliography.

The Tomb Builders

PRESENT archaeological evidence indicates that Ireland has been inhabited by man for about 9,000 years. The oldest known settlement site, at Mount Sandel beside the River Bann south of Coleraine, produced radiocarbon dates of 7000–6500 bc. Excavation revealed post-holes of ancient dwellings and a variety of artefacts used by Mesolithic (Middle Stone Age) hunters and food-gatherers.

It is of course possible that even earlier traces of man may yet be found, though it is unlikely that the island was inhabited before the end of the last Ice Age some 10,000 years ago. The land bridges formed between Ireland and Britain when the ice began to melt were of relatively short duration and had probably been submerged before the arrival of the first colonisers, who must have crossed over by sea, either in skin-covered boats or dug-out canoes. That living fossil, the Boyne coracle, and the sea-going curraghs of the west of Ireland, may have evolved from the boats of Mesolithic fisherfolk.

Mesolithic people led a semi-nomadic existence as dictated by their continual search for food. They lived in coastal campsites and beside river estuaries, possibly too on lake islands and may thus have been the instigators of crannog dwelling, a form of settlement which was to become widespread in the Iron Age and Early Christian period. Despite their long tenure of the country, Mesolithic inhabitants contributed little to the shaping of the landscape, being food collectors rather than food producers, and no structural monuments of their culture survive. They fashioned their primitive tools from flint, present in abundance in the layers of chalk underlying the Antrim basalts. Quantities of worked flints are contained in the 25-feet raised beach of the Curran at Larne, after which well known site Mesolithic culture has been given the name Larnian.

It was not until the arrival, early in the fourth millennium BC, of Neolithic (New Stone Age) settlers that the Irish landscape began to acquire a distinctive personality at the hand of man. The newcomers were the country's first farmers, they introduced crop production and animal husbandry, occupied permanent settlement sites, and built large and often spectacular tombs to their dead. These monuments are distributed in great number throughout the land and are by far the most impressive legacies of Stone Age enterprise. In the mid-nineteenth century the term 'megalithic' (from the Greek words *megas*, meaning great, and *lithos*, stone) was coined to describe them and has since found a permanent place in archaeological literature. It is today applied to a wide range of Neolithic and Bronze Age monuments, not all of which are by definition megalithic (certain types of prehistoric tomb, for example, are constructed with relatively small slabs of stone), though they probably belong to the same tradition.

Recent research has established that the Neolithic period in Ireland extended over nearly if not fully 2,000 years, commencing perhaps soon after 4000 BC and ending with the start of the Bronze Age early in the second millenium. The long held view that the different megalithic tomb types belong to more or less separate phases has had to be revised, and it now seems more probable that these monuments overlapped chronologically.

Irish megalithic tombs comprise a number of types but are broadly divided into two distinct classes, called gallery-tombs and passage tombs. To the first belongs the earliest type of burial monument so far identified, the court-tomb (or court-cairn, since many were originally mounded-over with a cairn of stones), consisting of a segmented gallery to hold cremated or, more rarely, inhumed burials. Almost without exception the distribution of court-tombs is confined to the northern half of the country.

The distinguishing feature of court-tombs, from which the type takes its name, is an open space or court in front of the gallery. The shape of the court is demarcated by upright slabs of stone called orthostats and may be semi-circular (forecourt type) or oval (fullcourt type) in plan. To the first the descriptive name 'horned-cairn' has been given, while the second is sometimes referred to as a 'lobster-claw cairn'. Generally the court is located at one end of the monument, to the east of the gallery, but variations are encountered in both types: some tombs have galleries opening onto both ends of a central court; or, in reverse arrangement, the tomb may consist of two long galleries set back to back with open forecourts at opposite ends, forming what is known as a dual-court tomb, as at Audleystown in Co. Down. It has been conjectured that the purpose of the court was to provide a ritual area in which the mourners assembled.

Tombs with large courts like Creevykeel in Sligo and Ballyglass in Mayo could therefore be presumed to reflect the social standing of the deceased.

Court-tombs in the east of the country generally have simple semi-circular forecourts— the classic Ulster 'horned-cairns'— while those in the west tend to be of more complex design on the fullcourt pattern. Whether this indicates an initial settlement in the east followed by a gradual spread into western districts, culminating in elaborate tombs like Magheraghanrush in Sligo, or whether in fact the movement was in the opposite direction, remains to be resolved.

Portal-tombs, popularly called 'dolmens', are single-chamber tombs of which there are about 150 examples known in Ireland. Before prehistoric burial monuments were classified into types, it was usual to refer to them as 'cromlechs', a misleading term that has long been out of favour. More recently the word dolmen has come to be associated with the large free-standing megalithic chambers of the portal-tombs. A loosely descriptive term rather than a recognised archaeological one, it is derived from the Breton word for a stone table. A frequent appellation in Ulster is *cloghogle*, a 'raised stone'. Countrymen also invented other, more colourful names: Giants' Graves, Druids' Altars, and Diarmuid and Grainne's Beds (after the fugitive lovers of ancient legend), and tend to regard them still with a respect founded on superstition.

Portal-tombs occur most frequently in the northern counties of Sligo, Donegal, Down and Tyrone. There are also some notable examples in south-east Ireland, and a few outliers are found in the far west, mostly around Galway Bay. In its basic form a portal-tomb comprises a chamber constructed of tall orthostats, across the tops of which rests a large roof-slab or capstone. Some of the simplest and at the same time most striking specimens consist of just three uprights and a capstone, and are designated 'tripod-dolmens'. It is usual for the paired front supports to stand higher than the back stone, thereby giving the capstone its characteristic uptilt while accentuating the entrance or portal features. There sometimes remains in position between the portal stones a tall door-slab which closes the chamber; in some examples a low sill-stone serves the same purpose. Capstones can be gigantic (one at Browne's Hill in Co. Carlow weighs an unprecedented 100 tons, unequalled anywhere else in Europe) and their emplacement must have entailed considerable labour and ingenuity. It was probably accomplished by hauling the stone up an earthen ramp constructed behind the chamber, using levers and rollers. That the capstones were positioned with an understanding of weight distribution seems evident since so many of them have remained securely aloft for several thousand years.

While a single chamber and capstone is usual, there are a number of twin-chambered examples suggesting possible affinities with the court-tombs. There is also a small group which have two capstones, a main one resting partially on a smaller one, as at Knockeen in Waterford and Kilmogue in Kilkenny.

Placing the dolmen structures in their proper chronological sequence poses problems. Their simple albeit dramatic forms could be interpreted as belonging to the primary phase of tomb-building, and this opinion was shared by many archaeologists in the past. Latterly, however, this view has been changing and the available evidence now seems to point to the dolmens having appeared comparatively late on the Neolithic scene, say around 2000 BC. It is possible that they may be degenerate versions of the court-tombs with which they appear to share certain features. One is tempted to regard them as representing a vigorous resurgence of the megalithic tradition among people who no longer built in the sophisticated manner of the multi-chambered court and passage-tombs.

Where large mounds or cairns survive intact they frequently cover passage-tombs. The cairn shape is round, distinguishing this type of monument from the more numerous gallery-tombs which are generally contained in long cairns. Passage-tombs, as their name implies, consist of a burial chamber or chambers reached by a narrow passage formed of upright slabs supporting a lintelled or corbelled roof. The ground plan of the chamber varies, circular, polygonal and cruciform shapes all being known.

Passage-tombs are often sited in commanding positions on high ground and sometimes cluster in groups— so-called megalithic cemeteries. Best known is the remarkable aggregation of tombs at the Bend of the Boyne in Co. Meath, of which the most celebrated monument is Newgrange, pre-eminent among the passage-tombs of Europe. Its beautifully decorated stones rank among the wonders of megalithic art. Now a major tourist attraction, surrounded by a protective fence and provided with an on-site information centre and ticket office, Newgrange has, like Stonehenge in Britain, lost some of its mystic atmosphere; but it remains imposing nevertheless, a glittering temple of the dead overlooking the green fields of Meath. The great curved façade, resplendent in its cladding of white quartz stones from the cairn-slip, is a conjectural reconstruction.

Though mysteries remain, painstaking excavation at Newgrange over many years has revealed some of its ancient secrets to the modern world. The most intriguing discovery, the significance of which eluded archaeologists for a time, was the existence of a stone 'roof box' above the entrance to the tomb. Eventually it was realised that its function was to allow the sun's rays to penetrate the dark alcoves of the burial chamber on the morning of 21 December, the winter solstice. Professor M. J. O'Kelly, who directed conservation work at Newgrange in the 1960s and 1970s, has witnessed the shaft of midwinter sun enter and illuminate the chamber during his lone vigils in the tomb. Evidently the builders of the monument possessed the necessary astronomical knowledge and planning skills to enable them to achieve a high degree of accuracy in its orientation, presumably resulting from careful observations at the site over a long period. The derided eighteenth-century antiquarian Charles Vallancey was not so wide of the mark after all when he called Newgrange 'the Cave of the Sun'.

But was this ingenious arrangement merely for the benefit of the dead? Or had it a more practical purpose bound up in ritual? Could it be perhaps, that the tribal hierarchy went into the chamber on the shortest day to observe the phenomenon and draw up a calendar for the coming year?

Another Boyne tomb, Knowth, is also proving exceptionally rewarding. Like Newgrange it has a wealth of decorated stones both inside and out, but one recent find is unique, a Neolithic 'mace-head', which is the only known piece of three dimensional carving of the period. Excavation work continues at the site and it will be some time before Knowth is open to public inspection.

Two miles south-west of Sligo town at Carrowmore is the largest concentration of megalithic tombs in Ireland, comprising many small passage-tombs of simple construction, the bold dolmen-like form of the chambers contrasting with the complex corbelling found in the Boyne tombs. Many of the monuments preserve only the megalithic chamber standing in isolation, others are ringed by massive boulder kerbs which presumably once formed the revetment of a cairn. These tombs owe their rugged architecture to the nature of the available building materials, huge granite boulders plucked from the slopes of the Ox Mountains by the advancing ice sheets of the last glaciation.

A denuded tomb at Cloverhill, about a mile to the east of the main Carrowmore group, has three of its stones decorated with curvilinear and lozenge motifs. This feature has helped to establish Cloverhill's identity as a passage-tomb and possibly link its designs with the megalithic art of the Boyne tombs. Cloverhill is however of special interest as decoration is otherwise unknown in the western passage-tombs.

One other passage-tomb cemetery, Carrowkeel, also in Co. Sligo, occupies a series of stark limestone ridges in the forlorn Bricklieve Mountains to the west of Lough Arrow. There are fourteen cairns, not all of which contain typical passage-tombs: one elongated example appears to have affinities with the court-tombs, possibly indicating a mingling of two cultural traditions. This important site has given its name to a type of pottery vessel peculiar to passage-tombs, called Carrowkeel Ware.

Towards the close of the Neolithic period a new type of gallery-tomb made its appearance and continued to be built in the ensuing Bronze Age. This was the wedge-tomb, so-called from its tapered shape, reducing in height and width from west to east and contained in a short, usually oval cairn. The tomb entrance characteristically takes the form of a small antechamber separated by jambs from the main chamber, behind which there may occasionally be another small closed chamber.

Wedge-tombs predominate in the west, but are well represented throughout Ireland with some 400 examples on record. The people who built them probably settled initially in the copper-rich lands of west Munster, whose deposits they may have exploited for commerce. Their culture is sometimes called Bell-beaker from the decorated pottery that has been found in these tombs. Wedge-tombs are numerous in Co. Clare and in the Burren region in particular where the local geology contributes to a symmetry of construction not achieved elsewhere. Sides and capstones are frequently squared limestone slabs, and the gallery is unsegmented, consisting of a single chamber. A feature peculiar to wedge-tombs (but absent from some of the Co. Clare variety) is the double walling of the chamber, utilising two parallel rows of orthostats. The outer wall does not appear to have a practical function as it is of lesser height than the inner one which bears the weight of the roofing slabs.

Whilst the megalithic tomb types discussed above testify to the building skills of prehistoric man, there were, as might be expected, less ostentatious modes of interment which left little or no trace. Cisted burials (small stone-built chambers containing cremated or inhumed remains and accompanied sometimes by urns and food vessels) were in widespread use from Neolithic times to the Iron Age. They occur both as single mound-covered graves and collectively in groups with no surface indications. Another type of burial monument, the ring-barrow, also tends to be inconspicuous, consisting of a low mound enclosed by a fosse and outer ring-bank. They too were in use over a long period.

◁ Kilclooney More, County Donegal (p. 19)

An exceptionally fine portal-tomb or
dolmen, prominent on the skyline ¼ mile
to the east of the main road, 4 miles
north-north-west of Ardara. It well
displays the classic features from which
this type of monument derives its name.
The matched portal stones and gracefully
uptilted capstone (nearly 20 feet long and
one of the largest in Ireland) oversailing
the chamber entrance convey a sense of
architectural awareness on the part of the
builders, and its streamlined profile has
inspired numerous analogies: a bird, a
fish, Concord, etc., depending on the
imagination of the observer.

The tomb is substantially complete. A
low sill-stone set between the 6-feet high
portals closes off the chamber entrance.
The lower end of the capstone does not
rest directly on the back-stone as is
usually the case, but is supported instead
by a small intermediate stone whose
function may have been to give increased
height to the chamber. Fragments of
undecorated Neolithic pottery were the
only recorded finds.

A short distance west of this tomb is
another of similar construction but on a
very much smaller scale. It is now partly
collapsed. A modern field wall separates
the two, which were evidently mounded-
over by the same east-facing cairn, traces
of which remain.

Carrowmore, County Sligo ▷

Distributed over many acres and extending
into adjoining townlands, Carrowmore
represents the largest grouping of
megalithic monuments in Ireland, an
immense Neolithic burial ground where
once there may have been more than a
hundred tombs. Casual exploration in the
last century and present-day gravel
quarrying in the vicinity have devalued
the archaeological potential of the site;
but it is still a rewarding place to visit,
steeped in atmosphere and evoking a
sense of the past. The surviving
monuments, some much more despoiled
than others, comprise truncated passage-
tombs whose megalithic character derives
from the huge ice-transported erratics
used in the construction of the chambers.

The equally massive kerbs of vanished cairns are sometimes mistaken for ritual stone circles, which they resemble. A number of the tombs here have lately been the subject of controversial dating by a team of Swedish archaeologists, whose findings suggest that they may have been built before 4000 BC.

To the north-west of the Carrowmore group rises the prominent hump of Knocknarea (1,014 feet), a cairn-crowned hill traditionally held to be the burial place of Queen Maeve of Connacht. The colossal cairn, 35 feet high and 200 feet across at the base, is much before her assigned period in the annals and illustrates the way in which folklore compresses time to accord with legend. Its siting and general appearance indicate a passage-tomb, though it has never been opened.

To appreciate what Carrowmore may have looked like originally, one must visualise this undulating countryside without modern houses, field-fences, roads and the pock-marks of gravel workings. The hundred or so monuments dotted

over this green landscape would have been more conspicuous then, many of them clearly seen from a single viewpoint as they were doubtless intended to be, a great necropolis spread out below Knocknarea, whose elevated cairn perhaps provided a focus for the tomb builders.

Goward, County Down △

Known colloquially as 'The Cloghmore' (Irish for 'great stone'), this prodigious monument fully lives up to the name. The corpulent capstone, 13 feet long and 10 feet wide, has an estimated weight of 50 tons and stands 14 feet high overall. This ponderous load has shifted sideways on its supporting uprights, possibly due to the collapse of the backstone, and now overhangs the chamber on its north side. The unsegmented burial chamber is 9 feet long with an entrance on the east, flanked by orthostats which could be the remains of a crescentic facade such as is found in the court-tombs, from which portal-

22

tombs, or dolmens as a class may have derived.

This extraordinary megalith has inspired a variety of descriptive names in the past, among them Finn's Finger (after the legendary giant Finn MacCoul of causeway-building fame), presumably on account of the tall slender upright stone at the front of the chamber; while to some of the older people of the neighbourhood it is Pat Kearney's Big Stone, so-called after the occupier of an adjacent cottage who for many years assumed the unofficial role of custodian of the monument. Pat Kearney lived here around the turn of the century and is of course long gone. So too is his humble house, now crumbled to its moss-covered foundations. Only The Cloghmore remains, dark and immutable in its tree-shaded field, a singular testimony to the enduring works of prehistoric man.

▽ *Knockeen, County Waterford*

One of the most spectacular megalithic tombs of the distinctive south Leinster group, a stately Neolithic mausoleum,

'remarkable,' to quote Borlase, 'for its solidity, and the perfect carrying out of a unity of design'. As a scheduled National Monument it is entitled to better care than it currently receives. It stands neglected in a corner of the disused burial ground of Kilburrin, 4 miles south-south-west of Waterford city, its great lichen encrusted stones emerging from a tangle of overgrown hedges.

The size of this monument is quite astonishing when viewed at close quarters and it is evident that considerable labour must have gone into its construction, perhaps over a number of years. The paired portal stones reach the imposing height of 9 feet and have a heavy door-stone set between them to close the porch-like entrance. There are two capstones, a feature peculiar to several portal-tombs in the area: the main one, a massive horizontal slab 12 feet long and 3 feet thick, rests on the portal stones and on the smaller capstone which covers the rectangular chamber. The overall height of the dolmen is 12 feet.

◁ *Magheraghanrush, County Sligo* (pp. 24–5)

Occupying a commanding hill-top overlooking islanded Lough Gill to the south and pretty Colgagh Lake to the west, this large and imposing monument is perhaps the best example of a centre court-tomb in the country. Its traditional name, by which it is still known hereabouts, is *Leacht Con Mhic Ruis*. The oval court, 50 feet in length with an entrance on the south side, has two segmented galleries at its east end and one at the west. In the last century all three galleries had large lintel stones resting across the portals, but two have since been removed. The remaining one, over the entrance to the north-east gallery, is fractured, the two halves held in position by inward pressure. These trilithon-like features were the cause of the monument being misleadingly labelled 'The Irish Stonehenge'.

The tomb is now surrounded by the trees of a young plantation of conifers and is screened from view until one arrives at it. On the hill below are other

antiquities including a wedge-tomb and a despoiled stone ring-fort with a roofless souterrain.

Proleek, County Louth △

A splendid 'tripod-dolmen', 12 feet in height, standing at the edge of a field near a ruined gallery-tomb. It is reached by a signposted path from the grounds of Ballymascanlon Hotel. It has long been called 'The Giant's Load' since, from a certain viewpoint, it resembles a huge figure bowed under the weight of a heavy burden—in this case a rounded granite capstone weighing in excess of 30 tons. This well known landmark has often been illustrated. As early as 1742 an engraving of it appeared in Thomas Wright's *Louthiana*, wherein he states that 'the native Irish tell a strange story about it, relating how the whole was brought all at once from the neighbouring mountains, by a giant called Parrah Boug

M'Shagjean, and who they say was buried near this place.' Unlike other antiquarians of his day, Wright recognised the sepulchral purpose of these monuments and dismissed as fantasy the idea that they were Druid's altars.

Visitors to Proleek will notice that the top of the capstone is dotted with pebbles: throw one up, runs the legend, and if it remains on the convex surface the person who cast it will marry before a year has elapsed.

△ *Legananny, County Down*

One of the most aesthetically satisfying megalithic structures of the Irish countryside, a 4,000 year-old Neolithic tomb that might equally be a work of modern sculpture. If proof were needed that Stone Age man built his monuments to impress as well as to last, then here it is. Its rugged geometry has long been admired, and illustrations of it have appeared in innumerable publications as well as in television commercials promoting tourism and butter. It was Fergusson who coined the term 'tripod-dolmen' to describe this and similar portal tombs, believing that it never had a covering cairn but was always intended to be seen as it stands now, 'a studied exhibition of a *tour de force*'. This is an opinion shared be some archaeologists today.

As with all tripod-dolmens, Legananny consists of just three uprights and a capstone. The dominant portal stones are some 6 feet high and the tapered back-stone 4½ feet. The smooth-topped granite capstone is 10½ feet long and characteristically uptilted at the front, decreasing in width towards the back of the tomb. Though it is somewhat off the beaten track, the megalith is well signposted and can be reached by car. Not least among the rewards of seeking it out in the stony acres of Cratlieve under Slieve Croob, are the splendid views of the Mourne Mountains far to the south.

Tawnatruffaun, County Sligo (p. 28, top) ▷

Known as 'The Giant's Griddle' and recorded as such on the ½-inch O.S. Map, this handsome megalith is fairly well preserved despite forming part of a modern wall into which some of the cairn

stones have been built. The chamber lacks at least one of its side stones, but the large capstone is still in position. A cup-marked stone is contained in the wall near the Griddle, and remains of a second tomb lie close by.

This monument is not easy to find without asking directions locally, nor is access to it straightforward since it is situated in bogland which often becomes waterlogged. But with suitable footwear it is well worth a visit, a peaceful and solitary site, with the long outline of the Ox Mountains dominating the view to the south. Some distance to the west, near Owenykeevan River but elusive in a vast tract of peat, are the Great and Small Griddles of the Fiana, two ruined gallery-tombs.

◁ *Creevykeel, County Sligo* (p. 28, bottom)

A magnificent, well presented full-court tomb, restored after excavation in 1935 and protected by a modern wall. One of the more accessible monuments of its type, it is situated at the rear of a cottage on the east side of the Bundoran-Sligo road, near the hamlet of Creevykeel.

The long cairn is wedge-shaped and tapers sharply towards the west. The court, 50 feet in length, has straight sides and shallow curved ends. It is entered by an orthostat-lined passageway on the east. At the west end of the court is the roofed entrance to a long gallery, divided by massive jambs into two chambers in which were found cremated burials and fragments of grave goods. In addition to the main gallery and to the west of it, are three small burial chambers set into the sides of the cairn. These are seemingly contemporary with the main tomb.

The orthostats flanking the entrance to the gallery are impressively large, several standing 6 feet high, whereas those lining the remainder of the court are of much lesser size. It has been suggested that this may indicate that the full-court tombs evolved from the open or forecourt type; though one might expect to find the largest stones occupying positions of importance in any case. In Early Christian times the monuments appear to have been used for domestic purposes, when a drying kiln was built in the court. Part of the walling of this structure survives.

◁ *Aughnacliff, County Longford* (p. 29)

One of a small group of portal tombs which have two capstones (others include Knockeen in Waterford, Kilmogue in Kilkenny and the Kempe Stones in Down). Like many 'dolmens' it stands in a hollow, so that the visitor's initial view of it is from above. The main capstone is 9 feet long and rests at the front on the single remaining portal stone, 6 feet high, on which a small Christian cross has been inscribed, apparently recently. The lower capstone is supported on the chamber uprights and, as it now stands, the whole presents an eye-catching study in balance.

▽ *Woodtown, County Dublin*

Although partly collapsed on its supports and overgrown with bracken and scrub, this is nonetheless a noble megalith. When complete it would have stood 15 feet high at the chamber entrance, where there now survives only the broken portion of one of the great portal stones, against which the massy capstone leans, its other end resting on the ground. A second portal stone nearly 15 feet long, lies fallen alongside.

Borlase believed this to be a distinct class of tomb—an 'earth-fast' dolmen, so-called from the capstone's contact with the ground at the back (another example being Howth dolmen in the same county). However, the term is not recognised in modern archaeology. It is of course possible that the back of the capstone was never raised up; but, as we have seen in other large monuments, such feats were well within the capabilities of Neolithic tomb-builders.

Access to this megalith, known also as the Mount Venus dolmen after the estate in which it stands, is through a gap in a hedge beside a golf course, about ¼ mile east of Woodtown road junction.

Kiltiernan, County Dublin ▷

Borlase graphically described this rather ungainly portal-tomb as 'a sphinx-like monster, advancing out of a rocky hill on some half-dozen short and rickety legs.' Its unusual shape immediately draws the

eye, and it stands out boldly in a field which has many natural formations of large boulders. The 40-ton capstone is 22 feet long and covers an elongated chamber which yielded coarse Neolithic pottery.

Immediately behind the tomb is a raised rocky ledge, and it has been suggested that the capstone was emplaced by sliding it from this onto the supporting uprights. The availability of a suitable slab of rock, especially a very heavy one, must have influenced the siting of many dolmens.

Carrickglass, County Sligo (p. 32) ▷

Surely the most bizarre legacy of the megalith builders, this unique Neolithic tomb, 'the Labby Rock,' has been called the clown among Irish dolmens. And not without reason, for there is something vaguely incongruous in the sight of its seemingly inadequate uprights straining under the inexorable weight of the 70-ton capstone. This is a massive limestone block 15 feet long by 9 feet wide and 8 feet thick, scarred with fractures and sprouting a shaggy growth of heather and grasses. How this colossal mass was lifted into position remains a mystery. Presumably it was raised *in situ*, for it is inconceivable that it could have been transported over any distance. The chamber underneath is oblong in plan and measures 6 feet by 3 feet; it has not been excavated in recent times, but cremated remains were removed from it in the last century. The tomb entrance is tightly closed with a door-slab set behind the portals, which the front of the capstone overhangs.

This somewhat hidden monument crouches at the bottom of a field behind a farmhouse, near the north-eastern end of Lough Arrow and about 4 miles west-north-west of Ballyfarnham. Like so many ancient structures in the Irish countryside it has been incorporated in a boundary wall.

31

△ *Srahwee, County Mayo*

This picturesquely situated wedge-tomb
preserves many of the classic features of
the type. The tapered form is well defined,
as is the double walling of the segmented
gallery, partially covered by a large flat
roof-slab. A door-stone closes the tomb
entrance, which faces west. There is some
indication of the existence of a cairn. The
monument stands by the roadside at the
north-east corner of Lough Nahaltora and
was in the past resorted to as a holy well
by local people.

Wedge-tombs were introduced in the
south-west of the country, probably by
newcomers from France around 2000 BC
at the close of the Neolithic period, and
continued to be built in the Bronze Age.

33

△ *Poulnabrone, County Clare*

The stark limestone uplands of north-west Clare embrace the area known as the Burren, a 100 square-mile region of immense botanical interest amongst whose colourful flora is to be found a wealth of antiquities. At first sight, one may wonder what enticement the burren (literally 'a rocky place') held for the first people who settled here, possibly in the Neolithic period. However, the harsh physical conditions we see today are of comparatively recent origin, partly the result of woodland clearance in prehistoric times, followed by widespread overgrazing which in turn led to erosion of the shallow soils by wind and rain. Only in the deep rock fissures was sufficient soil retained to nourish the rare Alpine and Mediterranean plants for which the Burren is justly celebrated.

Early man left his signature on this silvery-grey landscape in the form of wedge-tombs and portal-dolmens, none more striking in appearance than Poulnabrone, 5 miles south of

Ballyvaughan. Like many Stone Age sepulchres hereabouts, this familiar monument owes its neat constructional lines to the nature of the local materials. Solution acting on joints in the limestone causes the rock to split, producing the slender and often uniform slabs which distinguish these tombs.

Gortnavern, County Donegal (p. 35) ▷

This little known and somewhat difficult to find monument, 'Diarmuid and Grainne's Bed,' is located on a farm 1 mile south of Carrowkeel (*alias* Kerrykeel) village and about ¼ mile to the east of the road to Rathmelton. The portal stones are a well matched pair some 6 feet high, supporting the front edge of a craggy, cup-marked capstone which has been slightly displaced.

△ *Kilmogue, County Kilkenny*

Situated ½ mile west of the crossroads hamlet of Harristown and better known in the locality as *Leac an Scail*, this is the tallest portal-tomb in Ireland. The monumental entrance to the chamber consists of two majestic orthostats each 12 feet high, with a massive door slab set squarely between them. The pitch of the capstone is unusually steep and its front edge soars out over the portals to a point nearly 15 feet above the ground. It rests at the back on a smaller, secondary capstone, laid horizontally across the side stones of the chamber. The double capstone is found in a number of south Leinster tombs and elsewhere.

Because there is no officially recognised access to it, this noble megalith is unsignposted and forgotten, partly camouflaged by tall hedges in the corner of a field adjoining a farmyard, through which one must pass to reach it.

36

Foremost among the passage-tombs of Europe, Newgrange has long evoked the wonder of archaeologists and laymen alike. The most penetrating excavation work undertaken at any prehistoric site in Ireland so far has revealed much about its construction and purpose; but other secrets, such as the cryptic symbolism of its beautifully decorated stones, remain inviolate. The magnificent entrance slab—'one of the most famous stones in the entire repertory of megalithic art'—is especially satisfying, the confidently executed spiral and lozenge motifs still crisply defined after 5,000 years. The triple spiral, found only at Newgrange, occurs both on the entrance stone and inside the chamber. The passage is long, over 60 feet, and leads to a cruciform burial chamber with a corbelled roof which rises steeply upwards to a height of nearly 20 feet.

A revetment of large horizontal stones surrounds the base of the mound and many of these are also decorated with geometric designs. Formerly the mound was encircled by an outer ring of immense standing stones of which twelve remain.

Gaulstown, County Waterford (p. 38) ▷

The portico-like entrance to this megalithic tomb is a feature of a number of monuments in the Waterford district. Six uprights, including the east-facing portals and door-stone, comprise the tall chamber, which though closed at the front, can be inspected through a gap in the side. The capstone is a large craggy slab some 14 feet in length, scarred with crevices which provide a foothold for grass and mosses.

▽ *Cloghanmore, County Donegal*

A large tomb of the enclosed, full-court type, with parallel twin galleries placed at the western end of the court, each divided into two chambers. One of the galleries is roofed with a heavy capstone. Two small unsegmented chambers at the eastern end of the court have entrance stones decorated with curvilinear motifs recalling the megalithic art of the passage-tombs, but prolonged weathering has almost obliterated the designs.

The court is oval in plan and measures about 45 feet in length. An entrance passageway on the east is flanked by orthostats of monumental size. Much of the long tapered cairn survives, but owes its present form to considerable tidying-up of the monument in the last century. The site is situated in marshy ground and access is difficult in wet weather.

Haroldstown, County Carlow (pp. 40–1) ▷

Improbable though it may seem, this interesting megalithic tomb was lived in by a family in the nineteenth century, a purpose to which its large interior was suited and possibly to some extent modified. Gaps between the side-stones were windproofed with turf and mud, and no doubt the resulting 'house' was as snug as some of the tiny cabins occupied around the time of the Great Famine. The presence of a horse in the photograph is a reminder too that these ancient structures not infrequently served as animal shelters in the past. A visitor to the group of chamber tombs at Farranmacbride in Co. Donegal in 1871 records: 'On getting into another cavity, I found two black lambs inside, and in another some pigs, in another calves'.

Coagh, County Londonderry △

The Haroldstown dolmen stands near the bank of the Derreen River at Acaun Bridge, 4 miles north-east of Tullow. The chamber, 13 feet long and nearly 9 feet wide at one point, is more spacious than most portal-tombs and comprises about ten upright stones. There are two capstones, the larger of which measures some 12 feet in length. Between the portals is a tall door-stone to close the tomb entrance. Presumably the opening in the side of the monument is the result of one or more stones having been removed by the human tenants to gain access to the inside.

Though ignored by some guidebooks, this is a very fine megalith which unfortunately loses much of its impressiveness on account of the roadside hedge which threatens to envelop it. It has long been neglected and abused: a photograph taken in 1914 shows it defaced with auctioneers' posters; latterly it has become a target for religious graffiti.

The bulky granite capstone is 8 feet long and up to 5 feet thick and rests, somewhat precariously it would appear, on four of the six basalt uprights forming the chamber. The total height of the tomb is nearly 12 feet. Its local name, Tamlaght, means 'plague stone'; it is also known by the more common appellation Cloghogle, 'raised stone'. An account cited by Borlase states that several other dolmens formerly stood in close proximity here, possibly as an integral group of which the present monument is the sole survivor.

Stone Circles and Standing Stones

SINGLE standing stones or monoliths, called *gallan* in Irish, dot the countryside in countless number and come in all shapes and sizes. The taller examples are aptly described by another word in general use: *menhir*, a compound of two Welsh words meaning a 'long stone'. The best known Irish long stone, at Punchestown in Co. Kildare, rises to over 19 feet.

Standing stones are the most frequent monument type whose erection extended over a broad time span, commencing probably in the Neolithic period when the great stone tombs were built, and continuing into the Iron Age. Few have been excavated and dating evidence is scant. Some have been shown to mark Bronze Age cist-graves and it is likely that many were set up for purposes unconnected with burials, such as commemorating important events and indicating territorial boundaries. Other standing stones may have possessed a magical significance as prophylactic monuments.

The hole stones, too, of which several dozen are known, must have been more than grave markers or boundary posts. Their adoption in comparatively modern times as cure stones and for other obscure folk customs, some of which survived into living memory, may preserve elements of long forgotten pastoral traditions of great antiquity. In most examples the hole is circular, while a few have rectangular perforations, as at Tobernaveen in Co. Sligo, through which sick children were passed in the hope of effecting a cure. Fine hole stones may be seen at Doagh, Co. Antrim, Hurlstone, Co. Louth and Lackendarragh, Co. Cork.

Sometimes standing stones occur in groups which form no discernible pattern. At Timony Hills in Co. Tipperary several hundred are scattered over a wide area. Paired standing stones are not uncommon and have prompted male/female analogies. Standing stones arranged in straight lines are frequent in the counties of Cork and Kerry, and also in Ulster where they are usually found in association with stone circles.

Perhaps because they are the most mysterious of all prehistoric monuments, stone circles hold a particular fascination for many people. Often located in hauntingly lonely places well away from all signs of modernity, they can instil in the person who seeks them out a feeling of awe as he ponders their cryptic purpose. It is small wonder that these inscrutable rings of stone have in the past given rise to all kinds of bizarre speculation about their builders and users, arousing in the imaginative visitor visions of lurid torchlight ceremonies performed under the stars, presided over by robed druidic priests. That much may be fantasy. Equally, it is doubtful if we will ever come close to learning the truth about these monuments.

By definition, a stone circle is an arrangement of upright stones forming an open ring whose purpose was essentially ritual. It is often but not always megalithic in character. About two hundred sites are known in Ireland and it is probable that very many more lie undiscovered beneath large areas of blanket bog. Of the recorded sites two main concentrations are identified: in south-west Munster and mid-Ulster, the latter centred in the Sperrin Mountains region of Co. Tyrone. Here on the upland hill-slopes are numerous rings of low stones or boulders, frequently occurring in proximity as inter-related groups, but for all that inconspicuous among the monotones of heathery moorland. Stone circles are also found in the adjoining counties of Fermanagh and Londonderry and here too the stones tend to be of small size, generally no more than 2 feet in height. Some of the Ulster circles have associated stone rows, called alignments, and some stand near cairns and other burial monuments. All these features are present at Beaghmore, a remarkable Bronze Age ritual site uncovered in Co. Tyrone as a result of turfcutting activities.

Though the great majority of the Ulster circles consist of relatively small stones, there are one or two notable exceptions. The fine monument at Ballynoe in the Lecale Peninsula is truly megalithic, several of its closely set orthostats reaching heights of 6 feet. This circle is unusual in that it surrounds a burial mound, a combination which makes interpretation difficult.

Stone circles are scarce in eastern Ireland and only a handful of widely separated sites are recorded. In Wicklow is the well known Piper's Stones at Athgreany, and the lesser known but impressive embanked circle at Castleruddery. The adjoining county of Kildare has a ruined circle at Broadleas consisting of a boulder ring with raised interior. At Ballinvally on the north side of the Loughcrew Hills in Co. Meath, several huge stones delimit a circle with a diameter of about 70 feet.

The Munster distribution occurs mainly in two areas of

Co. Cork: one in the coastal district of Ross Carbery and its hinterland, the other in the Boggeragh Mountains some 30 miles inland. There is a wealth of stone circles in the hilly country to the north of Coachford, as well as many standing stones and alignments. The circles here are mostly of small diameter: Oughtihery $8\frac{1}{2}$ feet, Rylane $11\frac{1}{2}$ feet; but there are also some sizeable ones, like Loughatooma, an oval ring measuring 28 feet by 19 feet, and Gowlane North at 31 feet, unusual for the paired external stones forming a double portal.

Co. Kerry, too, has a good many sites, and several excellent examples are located along the east side of the Kenmare River. But though stone circles are so numerous in the south-west, only a comparatively small number are well preserved and readily accessible. Many survive as incomplete gorse and bracken-grown rings, unrecorded and long forgotten. Others have been overwhelmed by peat bog, leaving only the tops of their hoary stones peeping above ground to declare their presence. A few of the better known monuments are signposted, but while these include some fine megalithic rings like Drombeg in Co. Cork, there are other interesting sites which the dedicated hill-walker will only discover through personal inquiry. Some of the circles with the greatest sense of atmosphere are the most hidden, though they are not necessarily always remote from centres of population.

A distinguishing feature of many of the stone circles of Co. Cork is the presence in the ring of a horizontal axial stone, erstwhile referred to as a 'recumbent stone', aligned with two dominant portal stones placed directly opposite. This characteristic has led to a parallel being drawn with the axial stone circles of Aberdeen in Scotland, though there the arrangement of the stones is somewhat different. The occurrence of the axial stone has provided a strong argument in support of the theory that these structures were erected for an astronomical purpose. Other discoveries have strengthened this notion. Inside Kealkil stone circle near Bantry, excavators found channels in the ground crossing at right angles, marks which were interpreted as depressions made by timbers which could have supported, say, a vertical sighting post.

However, the popular idea that stone circles were sophisticated observatories built to the instructions of an astronomer-priest élite is now largely discredited. Attempts to establish precise celestial alignments for many of these monuments tend to be inconclusive, not because none could be discovered, but because those that were could not be shown to be the result of intentional planning.

The probability of fortuitous alignments occurring is high, and while some rings revealed several possibilities, others produced none. That is not to say that orientation played no part in the design of stone circles: on the contrary, it is noteworthy that the axial stone circles of west Munster are nearly always aligned north-east to south-west, that is, with the portal stones facing sunrise and the axial stone facing sunset. But there is sufficient deviation from one circle to another to suggest that exact alignment was not required and that orientation was more likely to be connected with ritual than with scientific study, perhaps in the same way that many Bronze Age wedge-tombs, with which stone circles are broadly contemporary, have their entrances facing south-west towards the setting sun.

The stone circles of south-west Ireland have diameters of from 8 to 30 feet or more. Small five-stone rings are the most consistent type and should perhaps be regarded as a specific class. There is a doubtful four-stone ring at Lettergorman in Co. Cork, the only known example in Ireland, though the type is common in Scotland. The larger axial stone circles of Munster are composed of between eleven and seventeen stones, while greater numbers are also found. The height and shape of the orthostats varies considerably, from low boulder rings whose stones are no more than a foot or so above the ground, to imposing circles like Bohonagh and Drombeg, the portal stones of which stand over 6 feet high. Both have diameters of 30 feet, typical for this region. Elsewhere there are a number of exceptionally large diameter circles, including two in Co. Limerick which span 150 feet. While the majority of stone circles are free-standing, some earth-banked rings occur, as well as enfossed examples which are related to the henge monuments.

It is clear that in some instances the stones were selected for their shape as well as their size. Mostly unworked slabs are used, often boldly faceted and aesthetically pleasing to the eye. Sometimes a natural feature may be emphasised by trimming and smoothing, and the stones may be graded for height, usually diminishing in size from the portals to the axial stone. Two of the stones at Drombeg are thought to be male and female symbols.

Cremated burials contained in unmarked pits have been found in several stone circles in Co. Cork. While this might presuppose a sepulchral purpose for these monuments it is more likely that the burials were of a dedicatory nature, a sanctifying of the circle in preparation for whatever rituals were to be performed there. In Co. Kerry a form of boulder-cist burial is fairly common and in a number of instances this is found in association with a stone circle, where it is placed at the centre of the ring. It typically consists of a large boulder capstone resting on a number of small stones, giving the appearance of a dolmen whose orthostats have sunk into the ground. Sometimes these structures are found outside the circle, as at Bohonagh, the capstone of which bears many cup marks. The presence of a boulder-cist may perhaps indicate the appropriation of a pre-existing stone circle for funerary purposes by a later cultural group importing new traditions. A number of stone circles in Cork and Kerry have a pillarstone of white quartz at their centre, again possibly introduced at a later date.

Sometimes what appears to be a stone circle is really the revetment of a despoiled cairn. Mention has been made in the previous section of the great boulder rings surrounding megalithic tombs at Carrowmore in Sligo: these must be regarded as the kerbs of denuded cairns rather than true stone circles, despite the similarity. On the other hand there are, as we have seen, stone circles composed of boulders, and the problems of positive identification are further complicated by the fact that some burial mounds are edged with standing stones which are evidently of far greater importance than a revetment, a ritual rather than a structural feature. O'Riordain has suggested that a possible origin of the free-standing stone circle might be sought in such burial monuments as Newgrange, with its surround of mighty stones, though no single explanation could be applied to all.

Reference has been made in passing to the henge monuments, a type of sanctuary consisting of a circular earthen bank with internal fosse. Some of these enclosures may pre-date the stone circle cult but others are probably contemporary with it, and a number of ritual monuments combine features of both (circle-henges). The massive earthwork known as the Giant's Ring near Belfast is evidently in the henge tradition though it has no exact parallel.

The most imposing of all the Irish stone circles is the Lios at Grange, by the western shore of Lough Gur in Co. Limerick. This well known and thoroughly investigated monument is composed of huge stones set contiguously inside a wide earthen bank. The monument is in some respects unique, but it fits within the accepted concept of stone circles as ritual centres rather than places of habitation, a fact which excavation helped to establish.

Northwards from Limerick stone circles are few and far between. At Moanmore East in Co. Galway is the curious Masonbrook Ring, *alias* The Seven Monuments, a circle of widely spaced standing stones 4-5 feet high, set on the rim of an earthen bank 70 feet in diameter. At Whitestream village, also in Co. Galway, is a circle of granite boulders, 58 feet in diameter, of which over thirty stones are still standing. There is a ruined megalithic chamber at the centre, a feature noted also in some of the Co. Kerry circles.

Several sites occur in Co. Mayo. At Rossport overlooking Bear Haven is a large double ring of stones, marked 'Druids Circles' on the ½-inch O.S. Map. Two stone circles stand on a hill-side close to Summerhill House, on the west side of Killala Bay. No fewer than four stone circles are to be found a short distance to the east of Cong village.

Two sites in Donegal merit description, each in its own way unusual. A megalithic ring 150 feet in diameter crowns the summit of Tops Hill 2 miles south of Raphoe. This large and confused monument is a combination of ritual stone circle and burial mound, the ransacked debris of which litters the interior of the ring, still impressive for the size of the remaining orthostats. Far to the north of here, scarcely a dozen miles from Malin Head, is the ruined but evocative stone circle of Bocan.

Standing stones which do not form part of the circle but which clearly have some association with it are found at a number of sites. Single and sometimes paired outliers can be conspicuously tall; at Mushera Beg in Co. Cork there is a great tilted pillarstone 12 feet high. Paired outliers are much less frequent than the single variety and can be seen at Lissyviggeen and Kealkil. A different feature is found at Gurteen near Kilgarvan in Co. Kerry, where two orthostats are set radially in front of the portals as if to emphasise the entrance, similar to the arrangement at Gowlane North, mentioned above. A five-stone circle at Lackaduv, to the north of Macroom in Co. Cork, has three outlying stones aligned on the axis of the ring through the recumbent stone.

Little has been said so far on the question of date. The few stone circles that have been excavated in Ireland produced hardly any datable evidence, with the exception of the Lios, the very ample finds from which enabled archaeologists to assign it with a fair degree of certainty to the Early Bronze Age. A similar date seems likely for Beaghmore, though there the evidence is somewhat diffused by the fact that it is superimposed on an earlier, Neolithic settlement. Perhaps the majority of stone circles do belong to the Bronze Age, though it is possible that a number were built as late as the Celtic Iron Age, which period may also have seen the utilisation of former sites for purposes other than those for which they were originally erected.

A clue to the uses of some stone circles might be sought

in folklore. The seven stones of Lissyviggeen are explained in an old legend as the children of two giants (represented by the tall outliers), all of whom were turned to stone as they danced. The theme of ossified dancers recurs in connection with other stone circles, both in Ireland and in Britain, and since folklore often preserves elements of fact, one might conclude that dancing in celebration of pastoral festivals figured in the rites practiced at these monuments, though this can only be part of the answer. Were stone circles complex astronomical observatories, or seats of judgement and law-making, or sacrificial altars, or, more prosaically, places of trade where bargains were struck and goods exchanged? In the end the mystery remains, tantalisingly locked in the stones themselves and in the lost culture of the people who painstakingly raised them into position over three thousand years ago.

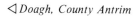
◁ *Doagh, County Antrim*

Rising picturesquely above a gorse-grown rocky outcrop, on the crest of a hill commanding a broad sweep of countryside, this shapely 'hole stone' is a good example of its type and a familiar landmark in the locality. Typical of places where the dumping of refuse is specifically prohibited, the immediate area abounds in unsightly litter.

A tapered dolerite slab about 5 feet high and 2½ feet wide at the base, it is pierced with a circular hole 3 inches in diameter, neatly cut, with smooth rounded edges on both sides. In the past betrothed couples joined hands through this aperture as a pledge of fidelity, a custom recorded in the *Dublin Penny Journal* in 1832, which also has a woodcut depicting the monolith.

This kind of monument is impossible to date, since like the far more numerous unperforated standing stones, they cannot be attributed to a particular period or culture. That they figured in local customs within living memory does not necessarily signify a lingering on of a prehistoric cult; though it is possible that some recently extinct folk traditions preserved elements derived from ritual practices of great antiquity.

Ardmore, County Donegal ▷

A squared pillarstone of monumental appearance, 7 feet high and 3 feet wide. Its south-eastern face is decorated with a profusion of cup-marks, many with single and multiple surrounding rings, a characteristic motif of the Galician or rock art of the Bronze Age. The stone is in a field behind a farmhouse, 1 mile north-north-east of Muff, to the west of the coast road to Carrowkeel and Moville.

In a low-lying field to the north (seaward side) of the road from Westport to Louisburgh and some 4 miles from the former, under the great mass of Croaghpatrick, are a number of megalithic remains. Though hardly conspicuous to the passing motorist, this interesting little group can be clearly seen from the roadside and is easily accessible. The main recognisable feature is a four-stone alignment which decreases in height from west to east, its largest stone standing about 4 feet above ground. There is also what appears to be part of a stone circle as well as several isolated standing stones, two of which rise darkly from peaty pools.

In view of the number of individual and associated stones in the group it is possible that this was a Bronze Age ritual site comprising stone circles and alignments, and perhaps burial monuments also.

Punchestown, County Kildare ▷

This gigantic monolith is the tallest and most remarkable of several 'long-stones' in Co. Kildare. Now standing 19 feet high, it was re-erected in 1934, having toppled from its tilted position three years earlier. Its overall length measured on the ground was 23 feet and its weight was calculated at 9.22 tons. A Bronze Age cist was uncovered at the foot of the monument. Many such pillarstones are thought to mark burials, but few have been excavated.

◁ *Bocan, County Donegal* (pp. 56–7)

A much mutilated but nonetheless impressive monument—one of only two stone circles recorded from Co. Donegal—situated on bleak Mass hill in the townland of Glack-na-drumman, a little over a mile from Culdaff village. Its ruinous state is largely the result of land clearance in the nineteenth century, when a number of its stones were overthrown and buried on the site. Either the operation proved unexpectedly troublesome, or superstition gained the upper hand, for the work was abandoned, leaving a dozen or so stones standing. Several more have been removed since, but sufficient remain to indicate a ring with a diameter of 65-70 feet, consisting possibly of 30 stones originally. The surviving orthostats are fine specimens up to 6 feet high. Like stone circles elsewhere, it has figured in the orientation debate: Somerville (1929) proposed an alignment on the summer solstice for it, with distant Farragan hill as a marker.

The site affords extensive views across the Inishowen peninsula, and this no doubt would have been a reason for its adoption in penal times as a place of clandestine Catholic worship: hence the name Mass hill. Anciently it was called Banchan, meaning a pasture, which it still is.

Longstone Rath, County Kildare ▷

A hauntingly esoteric site on a wooded hill in Furness estate, 3 miles east-north-east of Naas and 1 mile south-east of Johnstown. Though usually described as a rath, this is more properly interpreted as a ritual enclosure in the henge tradition. It consists of a circular earthwork nearly 200 feet in diameter, on top of and inside which are a number of mature hawthorn and ash trees. The bank, up to 9 feet high and cut by gaps on the east and west, is encircled by a fosse dug to a depth of 5 feet. The floor of the enclosure rises gradually towards the centre, at which point it is some 3 feet higher than the periphery. Excavations carried out in 1912 revealed that a fierce fire had burned over a large area of the interior, and this had subsequently been covered with a mound of earth and boulders.

Precisely at the centre of the ring and rising to the impressive height of 17½ feet, is a shapely four-sided granite pillarstone, socketed in a rock-cut pit and secured with packing stones. Its overall length is 21 feet, not far short of the similar monster at Punchestown a few miles away. Beside it is a long cist-grave in which were the cremated remains of two individuals, as well as pottery sherds and some items of ornament. No firm dating evidence is available, but the ring-work was probably constructed early in the second millennium BC and presumably belongs to the same general period as the ceremonial henges and sanctuaries.

Bohonagh, County Cork △

A large axial-stone circle, recently restored, standing on a breezy hill-top within a mile of the coast. Of its original thirteen stones nine remain: three of these were re-erected during excavation of the site in 1959. The diameter of the ring is slightly less than 30 feet and the axis runs east to west through the radially set portal

stones to the 'recumbent' or axial stone, resulting in an approximate alignment on the equinoctial sunset. Several of the orthostats on the east side of the circle are distinctly megalithic, and the matched portals exceed 7 feet in height, possibly the tallest pair of any Irish circle. This splendid monument is threatened by encroaching gorse.

A short distance to the east of the circle is a boulder-dolmen with a cup-marked capstone resting on low sandstone and quartz supports. The association of boulder-dolmens (or boulder-burials) and stone circles is known elsewhere, notably in the adjoining county of Kerry where they are usually placed at the centre of the ring.

Beaghmore, County Tyrone △

An ambiguous group of Bronze Age ritual and funerary monuments, overlying traces of Neolithic occupation in an area of cutaway bog to the south of the Sperrin mountains. Uncovered in stages since 1945, the structures comprise stone circles, tangential alignments and cairns, remarkable for their complexity and extent. It may safely be assumed that others await discovery beneath the all-pervading peat. As is usual in the Ulster circles, the stones here are mostly of no great height, with the exception of one ring which consists of quite tall orthostats; its interior is studded with several hundred low spiky stones of unknown significance, and it also has a diminutive cairn set in the perimeter. Only the alignments can fairly be described as megalithic, their angular boulders standing shoulder high in many cases. The cairns cover cists, in some of which cremated bone was found, and in one a porcellanite axe.

This unpromising landscape looked vastly different to the first Stone Age farmers who settled here, perhaps sometime in the fourth millennium BC. Clearances made in the forest cover supported crop production for several hundred years until the site was abandoned for agricultural use. In the early Bronze Age it became a ritual centre when the various monuments were built, possibly in separate phases. Eventually accumulating peat overwhelmed even the tallest stones and they remained concealed until our own day.

Beltany Tops, County Donegal △

The name of this solitary hill 2 miles south of Raphoe recalls the Celtic springtime festival of Beltane (the ancient equivalent of May Day), traditionally associated with the lighting of hill-top fires to regenerate the sun.

The wreckage of great stones on this well chosen site belongs to an earlier period than the Celtic Iron Age. As it stands, it poses problems of classification. Part stone circle, part mound, it has suffered at the hands of despoilers and must look very different from its original state. The enclosing ring is megalithic, several of its slabby stones attaining heights of 8 feet or more. Many lean haphazardly outward under the pressure of the disturbed, boulder-strewn interior, the surface of which is 3-4 feet higher than the surrounding land. A solitary outlier stands 70 feet to the south-east. Possible astronomical alignments have been suggested for some of the circle-stones: one, perhaps fortuitously, points to sunrise at or about Beltane.

△ *Eightercua, County Kerry*

Arrestingly sited on a ridge where it commands the attention of travellers on the road south-east of Waterville, this is one of the more accessible alignments in a county which affords several fine examples. Its four monumental stones, up to 10 feet in height, extend east to west for 30 feet. This appears to have been part of a more complex structure. There are traces of an enclosure, or possibly the base of a cairn, on the south side, as well as what looks like remnants of a megalithic tomb adjoining the alignment. According to local tradition, this is the burial place of the wife of Amergin, chief of the legendary Milesian invaders. It is interesting to note that the date given in the annals for their arrival in Ireland, c1700 BC, corresponds with the period to which one would expect this monument to belong.

Alignments, called stone rows in Britain, are well represented in the counties of Cork and Kerry, where perhaps fifty are known. They are usually built on elevated ground and often appear conspicuous on the skyline, which may have been a necessary part of their function. The number of stones varies but is generally between three and six, with heights of up to 12 feet and more. Alignments also occur in Ulster, commonly in association with stone circles, and contain many more—but appreciably smaller—stones than those in Munster.

The Lios, County Limerick ▷

Greatest of all the Irish stone circles, a remarkable megalithic ring set inside a wide earthen bank, now tree-shaded and overgrown, adding to its sense of wonderment. It stands near the western shore of Lough Gur in an area rich in antiquities. Those inveterate observers of the Irish scene, Mr and Mrs S.C. Hall, marvelled at these 'mighty vestiges of Druidical power,' accounting them 'the

most magnificent Druidical work, considered as a whole, that exists in the world'.

The Lios is an embanked circular setting of more than a hundred boulders and pillars enclosing an area 150 feet in diameter. The largest and most imposing stone is a gigantic conglomerate block standing some 8 feet above ground, believed to have been hauled to its present position from a source a mile away. The floor of the enclosure is covered with a deep layer of clay and gravel, apparently placed there to level the site and conceal

the small reinforcing stones inserted
around the bases of the orthostats. A
paved entrance passageway on the east is
flanked with uprights whose heights
conform to the slope of the bank, and
leads into the ring between a pair of
monumental portal stones. Excavation
produced no evidence of habitation or
burials, but did uncover a vast amount of
pottery, among it Beaker and Food Vessel,
which had been ceremonially broken.
That this was essentially a ritual site
seems incontrovertible. The available data
points to the monument having been

constructed around 2000-1800 BC.

In the next field to the north is a well
preserved free-standing stone circle, and
fragmentary remains of another.
Elsewhere the visitor will discover remains
of Stone Age houses, burial mounds and
cairns, standing stones, ring-forts and a
crannog. There is little signposting, so this
is a place for those who delight in
unhurried exploration.

Set in the verdant agricultural landscape of the Lecale peninsula, this large ring of ancient stones and the mound it encloses are of special archaeological interest. A combination of stone circle and long-cairn or barrow, its hybrid features are unknown elsewhere in Ireland and it may possibly be a multi-phase monument resulting from a mingling of different cultural traditions.

The circle has a diameter of 108 feet and is composed of about fifty-five stones set contiguously, some standing 6 feet high. Several have fallen and others may have been removed. The entrance appears to have been on the west where four large boulders form a kind of double portal, and there are a number of random outliers. A kerb-edged elongated mound in the eastern part of the circle covered a cairn with two cists in which were cremated bones; altogether the remains of seven individuals were identified. Also buried in the mound were a number of water-smoothed stones called *baetyls*, thought to have had a religious significance. The discovery of a pottery sherd of Carrowkeel Ware points to a date in the late Neolithic period, which if contemporary would place Ballynoe near the beginning of the stone circle cult.

The Giant's Ring, County Down ▽

Four miles south of Belfast in the townland of Ballynahatty, on a plateau overlooking the River Lagan, is the largest prehistoric ritual enclosure in Ireland. A circular earthwork up to 12 feet high surrounds an open space nearly 600 feet in diameter and some 7 acres in area. Five 'entrance' gaps, not all of which are presumed to be original, give access to the interior of the ring, and a few lone trees break the skyline along the rim of the bank. The ground inside the enclosure is somewhat higher at the centre, rather like an inverted saucer, evidently the result of earth having been removed from round the edge to provide additional material for the construction of the bank. Placed slightly off centre in the ring is a megalithic chamber with passage-tomb affinities, consisting of five orthostats supporting a tilted capstone. If there was

a covering cairn no trace of it remains. While not necessarily contemporary, both tomb and earthwork are probably of late Neolithic date.

In more recent times it is recorded that The Giant's Ring served as a venue for horse races, while nowadays it is a favourite haunt of picnickers and dog-walkers. It is by any reckoning a tremendously impressive place, a silent arena which holds the secrets of forgotten ceremonies of 4,000 years ago. From the top of the bank one has extensive views across suburban countryside to the high-rise buildings and shipyard gantries of an industrial city; but from the floor of the enclosure the sights and sounds of modernity are shut out and the only sense of movement is from the clouds overhead.

△ Drombeg, County Cork

Regarded as the exemplar of the West Cork stone circles, Drombeg, *alias* 'The Druid's Ring,' is a well preserved, clearly signposted and frequently visited monument. Its diameter of 30 feet is typical of several stone circles in the Ross Carbery district, all situated within a few miles of the coast. The circle is of the so-called recumbent type, with an axis running north-east to south-west, as with many of these monuments, providing an alignment on the mid-winter sunset. Of its seventeen stones, the tallest are the matched portals in the north-east quadrant, standing some $6\frac{1}{2}$ feet high. The recumbent, or, more correctly, axial stone, directly opposite, is a cup-marked boulder with a flat upper surface. The orthostats on either side of it are graded for height and have bevelled tops. A degree of symmetry is not unusual in stone circle design, but in the case of Drombeg it is very marked, suggesting that this was important to its ritual function.

The site was excavated in 1957, when the cremated remains of a youth were found in an urn buried in a central pit. Radio-carbon tests produced unexpected—though inconclusive—results, initially giving a date in the first century bc, afterwards revised to ad 480-720, well outside the generally accepted period for these structures. This does not necessarily mean that stone circles were still being erected in early Christian times. It is quite possible that a pre-existing Bronze Age monument was adopted for ceremonial purposes by Celtic peoples, in which case the burial may have been of a dedicatory nature. The proximity of an Iron Age domestic site a short distance to the west of the circle, consisting of hut foundations and a communal cooking pit and hearth, can hardly be unconnected even if the two are unlikely to be contemporary.

▽ *The Piper's Stones, County Wicklow*

The notion that people could be turned into stone in punishment for some misdemeanour or other is a recurring theme in Gaelic folklore, and here at Athgreany in the stillness of the Wicklow hills is a strange troupe of dancers and a piper, all ossified on the spot for violating the Sabbath with their merrymaking.

The circle stands on the crest of a low hill and consists of fourteen granite boulders and an outlier (representing the luckless piper) 40 yards to the north-east.

The tallest circle-stones are on the east: one of these measures 6 feet 4 inches in height and has a girth of over 12 feet. An old thorn tree grew on the circumference of the ring until it was recently blown down, and it now lies decaying among the timeless stones. Townland names frequently hold clues about past associations between places and traditions. Athgreany translates as 'Field of the Sun,' leading one to the conclusion that this was formerly a ceremonial site.

Not many miles to the west in the adjoining county of Kildare, there is another Piper's Stones, a much-ruined monument enclosed by an earthen bank.

△ *Reanascreena, County Cork*

Situated at a height of 570 feet above sea level and 3 miles inland from Ross Carbery, rush-stifled Reanascreena is a little known megalithic ring of twelve uprights and an axial stone. It is surrounded by a 12-feet wide fosse with an external earthen bank, a rare feature which suggests close cultural links with the henge monuments. A comparable but smaller embanked stone circle is at Glantane East in the same county.

When the Reanascreena site was scientifically examined in the early 1960s, it was found that peat had formed over the original floor of the circle and fosse, a process likely to have started in the last millennium BC, when bog growth accelerated as a result of changing climatic conditions. The ground in the vicinity of the portal stones showed evidence of erosion, thought by the

excavator to have been caused by repeated trampling over a long period; so that the users of the circle had found it necessary to reinforce this area with small boulders to prevent the orthostats from falling. Seemingly prehistoric peoples had habitually danced or walked here in observance of some ritual. As at Drombeg and nearby Bohonagh, cremated bone was discovered in a pit within the circle. Dating evidence is lacking, but this class of monument has its origins in the late Neolithic or Early Bronze Age.

The Celtic Legacy

THE introduction of ironworking around 300 BC, perhaps earlier, is associated with the arrival in Ireland of invaders versed in new techniques of weapon manufacture and accomplished in the decorative arts. The concept of an evolving 'Celtic' landscape peopled with the heroes of the early sagas has its roots in the centuries that followed, and is enshrined in such place-names as Tara, Navan, Dun Ailline and Rathcroghan. These royal residences and inauguration sites witnessed the great hostings of the Irish kings and princes in the Early Iron Age.

Closely related to these celebrated sites are the hill-forts, large earth or stone-walled enclosures encompassing many acres of a hill-top. One of the finest Irish hill-forts, the largest example of its class, is Mooghaun near Shannon Airport in Co. Clare, an immense triple-ring fortification some 27 acres in extent. Though nominally circular, these enclosures tend to be irregular in outline since the defences conform to the shape of the slopes they girdle. In fact, the proper name for these structures—contour hill-forts—describes them very well. This type of Iron Age monument is sparsely represented in Ireland, in contrast to Britain where hill-forts are far more numerous.

A highly distinctive Celtic art style called La Tène, characterised by abstract curvilinear designs, reached Ireland from the continent around 300 BC. Isolated examples of La Tène have been found on weapons and items of ornament, but the style is best known from a small, unique group of decorated stones of which Turoe in Co. Galway is the most famous.

The beginnings of Irish figure sculpture are hidden from us. The earliest subjects may have been carved stone heads which seem to have held a potent symbolism for the Iron Age Celts. Several well preserved specimens are displayed in the National Museum in Dublin but cannot be closely dated. It is probable that this kind of three-dimensional sculpture developed some time after rather than before the first century AD. A few surviving pieces, like the little horned Tandragee figure in Armagh Cathedral and the cryptic idols

71

of Boa Island in Co. Fermanagh, are perhaps best interpreted as Celtic deities.

Concentrated mainly in the southerly counties of Waterford, Cork and Kerry, with isolated examples occurring also in the north, are numerous standing stones bearing inscriptions in Ogham. This archaic form of Irish script is derived from the Roman alphabet and evolved in the late Iron Age, around AD 300, remaining in use until the end of the seventh century. Letters of the alphabet are represented by groups of lines arranged across, above and below a stem line, customarily the edge of a pillarstone. Most of the inscriptions are commemorative and give the name of an individual together with brief details of his forbears. Many of the better preserved inscriptions can be translated using the Ogham key, but unravelling their meaning is a task for the expert.

The field monuments most closely identified with Celtic Ireland are the scattered ring-forts which survive in astonishing number. In his penetrating survey of ancient fortifications in 1901, T.J. Westropp put the total number of known sites at around 28,000, of which the province of Munster claimed the largest share with 12,232, next being Connacht with 7,593. Westropp's calculations were based on forts marked on the large-scale O.S. Maps, and, as he himself recognised, was clearly an underestimate as a great many had been obliterated over the centuries.

Ring-forts, generally called *raths* when constructed of earth, *cashels* and *cahers* if stone-built, were in the main the defended homesteads of ordinary farming people. The simplest type of structure, which also provides the greatest number of examples, was a single bank enclosure that fulfilled a purely domestic role and was in essence the equivalent of the wall around a modern-day farmyard. Some influential chieftains occupied large stone cashels with terraced ramparts incorporating concealed passageways and guard chambers, the whole encircled by a series of concentric ring-walls for additional security. These complex structures may be presumed to have had a quasi-military purpose.

Around the larger ring-forts, those of wealthy farmer and warrior chieftain alike, there might also be several smaller satellite raths in which cattle were penned at night to protect them from marauding wolves and rustlers. Cattle raiding was practised on a large scale in the Celtic Iron Age; it provides the central theme of the epic saga of the *Tain Bo Cuailnge*, and may have been the reason behind the construction of travelling earthworks like the Black Pig's Dyke, which supposedly traverses the country from south Armagh in the east to the Sligo-Donegal border in the west, and is said to define the ancient territorial boundary of Ulster.

Discontinuous sections of the bank can still be traced in
Monaghan, Cavan and Leitrim, but it is unlikely that it ever
formed an unbroken line of defence.

Some ring-forts are believed to date from the Bronze Age,
and it is possible that this type of settlement may have
originated even earlier. But the great majority are much
more recent and most excavated examples belong to the
early Christian period. Occupation of many continued into
Medieval times and beyond, and it is not unusual to find
mortar-built castles and tower houses inside them. O'Brien's
Castle on Inisheer, Co. Galway, Rahinnane Castle in Co.
Kerry and Desmond's Castle at Adare, Co. Limerick, all
stand within old ring-walls.

Ring-forts are found in every county and in a wide variety
of terrain. Many of the pastoral raths are situated about the
margins of uplands, while large forts of evident military
importance are often built in prominent positions
commanding sweeping views of the surrounding
countryside—like Dun Eoghla on Inishmore, Co. Galway, a
strong circular cashel sharing the highest ground on the
island with a nineteenth-century lighthouse.

A typical earthen ring-fort consisted of a bank enclosing a
level, usually circular or oval area inside which stood the
houses of the occupants. The enclosed space might be as
little as 60 feet or as much as 200 feet in diameter. Where
there is now only a gap to indicate the entrance, there
would originally have been a wooden gate, perhaps with
palisading flanking the passageway leading to the interior.
Sometimes a more substantial entrance was required: that at
Cahervagliar in Co. Cork is formed of large slabs of stone,
creating an impression of permanence, while the bank itself
is composed of earth and rubble. In most cases the material
for the bank was obtained from a fosse or ditch dug round
the outside, an effective and economical way of exploiting
available resources with minimum effort. It will be apparent
to anyone looking at these works today that the banks have
been reduced in height by collapse of material into the fosse,
with the result that the defences present a much gentler
profile than when first constructed. Many raths have been
virtually levelled and barely show up against their
surroundings. Earthworks of this kind, however indistinct on
the ground, are often clearly revealed by aerial survey which
enables them to be studied in relation to other landscape
features. Old field patterns, some of which may be pre-Celtic
in origin, have been discovered in this way even when the
land has been repeatedly ploughed and superimposed with
later walls.

In contrast to the slight remains, other ring-forts survive
much as they started out, deeply enfossed banks which can

still impede access. Steep fosses exist at Ballycatteen in Co. Cork and Ardagh in Co. Limerick, though the latter appears never to have been completed. Some of the larger forts have several concentric ring-walls, a usual type being the trivallate or triple-walled rath, while a few have as many as five walls. Bivallate Tullaghoge in Co. Tyrone is a somewhat idiosyncratic example, but it well illustrates the more substantial enclosures which served as clan centres up to the Middle Ages.

Small earthen ring-forts are very widespread and one does not have far to travel in rural areas to find examples. A good place to see numerous small domestic raths is Ballymote in Co. Sligo, where they are located in roadside fields around the village. The Co. Down countryside in the vicinity of Scarva also abounds in raths.

Some ring-forts have features which may cause them to be mistaken for motte-and-bailey defences, a type of earthwork introduced by the Anglo-Normans in the late twelfth century. The prominent mound at Kilfinnane looks like a motte, but is almost certainly an Irish construction as it is encircled by a series of banks and fosses in the manner of the indigenous raths. The absence of an adjoining bailey is further confirmation of its native origin. Similar enfossed mounds occur elsewhere and are known as platform ring-forts, one of which, Ballingarry Down, also in Co. Limerick, provided its excavators with evidence of several well defined periods of habitation extending over many centuries. This had been a mature site at least 300 years before the arrival of the Anglo-Norman invaders, and possibly for much longer than that.

Stone-built ring-forts are as might be expected most numerous in western districts where the builders had an abundance of ready-to-hand materials. The massive forts of the Aran Islands are well known, especially Dun Aengus, possibly the most famous of all Irish defensive works. The limestone karst of north-west Clare is littered with stone forts, most in a ruinous condition having been plundered for building stone at various times, but several remain substantially complete and preserve interesting features and associations. Cahercommaun, a large trivallate fort poised on the edge of an inland cliff, was excavated in 1934 and dated to the ninth century. The foundations of stone huts and a system of underground passages were uncovered, as well as copious refuse deposits consisting largely of ox bones. Other finds included a silver brooch, wooden vessels and various tools.

Fosses are not as a rule associated with stone ring-forts, presumably because of the problems of excavating a ditch in rocky ground. A few rock-cut fosses are known, however, like the splendid example at Doon in the west of Co. Clare. In the same county is Cashlaun Gar, skilfully sited on a steep-sided knoll which fulfils the function of a fosse. A rare defensive feature of a small number of Irish forts is the *chevaux de frise*, an abattis formed of sharp stones set on end around the cashel wall. It is found, *par excellence*, at Dun Aengus, Co. Galway and at Ballykinvarga in Co. Clare.

An intriguing addition to many raths and cashels is the occurrence of underground passages, called souterrains, in the interior. They vary enormously in shape and complexity, from short straight tunnels, to ingenious arrangements of interconnecting ones with obstacles and dead-end diversions to confuse intruders. The most usual building method employed stone slabs for the walls and roof, though timber was sometimes used as a roofing material in both stone and clay-walled souterrains. Ogham stones were often appropriated for lintels, and their presence in souterrains can be a useful guideline for dating these structures. Ogham script came into use around AD 300, and it follows that the stones could only be included in the fabric of souterrains built after that time. Most are in fact likely to belong to the Early Christian period.

Whilst it is evident from the nature of some souterrains that they were places of temporary refuge, and in a number of cases even habitations (this has been deduced from the discovery of charcoal hearths and other signs of domesticity), others were used solely for storing perishable foodstuffs in cool conditions. Stone-built niches in the walls of derelict nineteenth-century cottages at Slievemore in Achill Island are reminiscent of the lintelled chambers of some thousand-year-old souterrains, illustrating how ancient building methods persisted in remote parts of Ireland until recent times.

Along the mainland and island coasts of the Atlantic seaboard, cliffed headlands afforded suitable sites for defence, a ditch dug across the landward approach and topped with a bank being all that was required to secure the position against attack. An off-shore rock stack might be adopted for the same purpose. Because of the simplicity of construction in many instances, promontory forts, as this type of defence is called, can be disappointing for the general visitor, often having nothing to show other than vestiges of scarcely recognisable earthworks; though they frequently compensate with magnificent views of cliff and ocean. Some are in such wild, exposed places that it is impossible to visualise them as other than temporary retreats to which isolated groups resorted in times of danger. Since most promontory forts lacked a fresh water supply they were probably not intended for continuous occupation.

The frequency with which the placename elements *dun* and

doon are encountered on the west coast indicates just how numerous these structures once were. Storms and cliff erosion have swept away all trace of many, but extensive remains can be seen at a number of locations, including Dun Bunafahy and Dun Kilmore at Achill in Co. Mayo, Dubh Cathair on Inishmore, Co. Galway, Carrigillihy at Glandore harbour, Co. Cork, and Dunbeg in the Dingle Peninsula. Although associated with coastal districts, promontory forts are also found inland, notable being Caherconree at 2,000 feet in the Slieve Mish Mountains in Co. Kerry.

A different type of fortification to any of the foregoing was the *crannog*, a habitation built on an artificial island in the shallows of a lake. A variety of materials provided the foundation: logs, stones, peat, brushwood, and even the bones of animals, compacted and secured with stakes driven into the mud on the lake bed. Predominantly, however, timber figured in the construction of a crannog, and from this characteristic comes its Irish name, from *crann*, a tree. On top of the island thus formed stood the house, surrounded by a palisade.

Lake-dwellings were homesteads of individual family groups. A remarkable aggregation of several hundred sites was discovered at Lough Gara in Co. Sligo in the early 1950s as the result of a drainage project. Excavation yielded numerous artefacts of Bronze and Iron Age date. The foundation logs of one crannog were shown to have been laid down by Mesolithic fisherfolk. The sites examined had been used over a lengthy period and built up with successive layers to new levels by later occupants. Crannogs have proved to be a rich source of antiquarian finds because the damp peaty conditions of such places are conducive to the preservation of normally perishable articles.

Other lake-dwellings utilised natural islands, the shoreline defended by a wall of drystone construction. Several walled islands occur in the Connemara lakes and there is an extremely fine example in the moorland above Fair Head in Co. Antrim.

△ *Dunbeg, County Kerry*

An Iron Age promontory fort, one of the most sophisticated monuments of its class, remarkable for the ingenious nature of its defences. It stands on a V-shaped headland in the south-west of the Dingle peninsula and while not difficult of access is unsignposted because of its hazardous condition, to which warning notices on the site draw attention.

The position of Dunbeg is very exposed and parts of the cliff have been severely eroded, carrying sections of the masonry into the sea. The landward defences consist of a massive drystone wall almost 150 feet in length, extending in a roughly east to west direction across the promontory. A series of earthen banks with intervening fosses form a complex outworks. The most noteworthy feature of the fort is its entrance. Of it Macalister wrote in 1898: 'in the whole of the earlier architecture I know of no more remarkable work than the imposing entrance through this great wall.' It remains much as he saw it; the passageway is about 20 feet long, roofed with large lintel stones and guarded by flanking sentry chambers contained in the thickness of the wall. The chamber on the west side is provided with a horizontal shaft to house a heavy wooden beam which could be shot across the passage as a barrier if the outer door was breached. A souterrain underlies the approach gangway through the banks and emerges some distance to the north of the wall. One can imagine a situation in which the besieged occupants made use of this tunnel to surprise their attackers from behind.

◁ Tullaghoge, County Tyrone

Probably an Iron Age sanctuary
originally, this was later to become the
inauguration place of the O'Neill
chieftains of Tyrone. Here at the clan seat
of O'Hagan, hereditary stewards to the
O'Neills, the ceremony was conducted in
the presence of the assembled under-
chiefs, with the recipient installed in an
ancient stone chair said to have been
blessed by St Patrick. The Great Hugh
O'Neill was himself thus enthroned at
Tullaghoge in 1593. That the inauguration
chair, a rough construction of stone slabs,
was in existence as late as the beginning of
the seventeenth century is known from a
contemporary map which depicts the chair
on the hill below the fort; this accords
with an account of it having been broken
on the orders of Lord Mountjoy in 1602,
a year before the collapse of the earldom
of Tyrone.

The fort, one of the last important clan
seats of Gaelic Ulster, is in essence a large
bivallate rath. It commands the summit of
a rounded hill, 2 miles south-south-east of
Cookstown, to the east of the
Stewartstown road. A double vallum with
an unusually wide and level intervening
fosse rings a central habitation area of
about 100 feet in diameter. The entrance
through the now heavily wooded banks is
a well defined passageway on the north
side of the enclosure. Of the thatched
cottage-style dwellings shown on the 1600s
Bartlett map no trace remains.

Cahermacnaghten, County Clare (p. 80) ▷

Although ring-forts of earth and stone
had their origins in pre-history, possibly
in the Bronze Age, this type of enclosed
settlement continued in use for a very
long time and became very numerous in
the early Christian period. Some, indeed,
were rebuilt or extended in the Middle
Ages as defensible homesteads even
though by that time mortared castles and
tower-houses dominated the countryside.

Cahermacnaghten, 4 miles east-north-
east of the spa resort of Lisdoonvarna,
was occupied as late as the end of the
seventeenth century and for some time
previously had been the teaching centre of
a celebrated Gaelic law school conducted
by the O'Davorens. A deed of 1675 shows

that it was then inhabited and lists the dwellings standing inside the cashel, which has a diameter of just under 100 feet, as well as other property outside the wall. Of these structures only unintelligible fragments remain, but the well built cashel is substantially intact and has remains of an interesting late medieval two-tiered gateway. The accumulation of centuries of domestic materials has raised the ground level inside the fort, covering the foundations of buildings whose outlines can still be detected on the present surface.

Lough-Na-Crannagh, County Antrim ▷

The custom of building lake-dwellings or crannogs may have started with the Mesolithic hunters and food-gatherers who arrived in Ireland 9,000 years ago, though no example excavated so far has been dated earlier than the Bronze Age. Most in fact appear to belong to the Early Christian period, and doubtless many were inhabited well into Medieval times and beyond.

Lough-na-Crannagh, a small limpid lake cradled in a hollow on the summit of Fair Head on the north Antrim coast, contains perhaps the finest walled crannog in the country. Its remarkably well preserved state may be the result of its onetime remoteness, but it is also likely that it was occupied until very late on and could have seen several phases of reconstruction at the hands of successive newcomers. The secluded situation is typical of the dispersed settlement pattern of Celtic Ireland and the site would have been an attractive one down the centuries.

△ *Staigue, County Kerry*

Most famous of the great circular stone
cashels, Staigue is also one of the best
preserved and conveys a fair idea of how
the larger Iron Age fortifications must
have looked in their day. A building
combining exceptional strength with
unexpected architectural flair, it was
plainly more than a vernacular ring-fort.
It invites comparison with the Grianan of
Aileach in Donegal, with which it shares

certain features, and like it may have been
a royal residence in the last pre-Christian
centuries. Its secluded situation, ringed by
a ridge of hills at the head of a narrow
valley with a view south to the coast, is
very beautiful.

The cashel wall is notable for its
uniformity. The stones are skilfully laid,
without mortar; the wall, 13 feet thick at
the base, rises with a pronounced batter
to a maximum height of 18 feet. At
intervals round the inside of the fort an

(detail) ▽

elaborate arrangement of ten flights of steps gives access to the top of the rampart. The south-facing entrance is a 6-feet high passage roofed with massive lintels, the jambs typically converging in the Irish manner. A fosse and ring-bank surround the cashel, adding to its considerable defences.

The technique of dry-walling so well demonstrated here has a long tradition, being found in Neolithic chamber tombs of 5,000 years ago. The survival of so many early structures throughout the Irish countryside is partly due to the mastery of the craft of interlocking stones to achieve total stability, even in large building works like Staigue. The tradition is carried on today on a lesser scale, in the building and maintenance of mile upon mile of field-walls in the rural west.

△ *Ballykinvarga, County Clare*

An exceptionally interesting though sadly
defaced cashel, 1 mile north-east of
Kilfenora. The ring-wall encloses an oval
space 150 feet by 130 feet and survives to
a height of 12 feet or so. Although
incomplete it shows a fair standard of
building work, incorporating unusually
large blocks of stone in the construction
of its lower courses. An abundance of
easily quarried limestone accounts for the
remarkable number of stone forts in the
Burren (about 500 are known in an area
of 100 square miles), indicating a sizeable
Iron Age population here.

Ballykinvarga has the rare feature,
confined to three or four Irish forts, of an
encircling *chevaux de frise* of sharp stones
set upright in the ground and extending as
a defensive ring for a distance of about 50
feet out from the cashel. Its onetime
effectiveness against intruders can be
readily appreciated by today's visitor,
since to venture across it without due care
is to risk a sprained ankle or grazed shin;
how much more hazardous, then, must it

have been for attackers advancing under a
hail of missiles hurled by the occupants.
The only unimpeded access to the interior
is on the south side where a passageway
leads through the *chevaux de frise* to an
entrance in the cashel wall.

The approach to this fort from the road
is itself a veritable obstacle course only to
be recommended to the nimble, as it
involves clambering over several field-
walls built of precariously balanced
stones.

Caldragh Idol, County Fermanagh ▷

An early, possibly one of the oldest extant
examples of Irish figure sculpture,
standing forlornly in the gloom of an old
burial ground near the south-west shore
of Boa Island in Lower Lough Erne. It
depicts two dwarfish figures gazing in
opposite directions and probably
represents a Celtic deity. But while the
influence of the pagan Iron Age seems

unmistakable, it is doubtful if the carving can be as early as the first century AD date sometimes claimed for it. Nonetheless, the stone evidently personifies an ancient pre-Christian cult which may have survived here in isolation into the Dark Ages.

The idol is 29 inches high and comprises two back-to-back figures with disproportionately large heads and flat pointed faces. The coarse features are delineated by boldly incised lines, the eyes wide and expressionless, the mouths open. The arms are crossed diagonally in front of the belt-girt torsos, on one of which a phallus is indicated. On the top of the stone is a shaped cavity, 5 inches deep, usually interpreted as a slot to receive a missing part of the sculpture, such as an antlered headpiece, if it is not a receptacle for blood offerings.

Close by is another carved figure, brought here from Lustymore Island. It may be broadly contemporary with the Caldragh Idol and like it represent a deity. Whatever their origin, there is something inescapably baleful about these stone dwarfs in their dank lakeside setting, surrounded by dark weather-worn slabs under the trees.

△ *Dunloe, County Kerry*

Turoe, County Galway ▷

Seven of the eight Ogham stones in this group were discovered in a souterrain at Coolmagort in the nineteenth century and have been set up on this site close to Dunloe castle. The tallest stone is 8 feet high. There is also a prostrate slab taken from the grounds of nearby Kilbonane church.

Ogham stones were frequently used as lintels in the construction of underground passages. Because of their long protection from exposure, the Dunloe inscriptions are unusually well preserved. All are of a commemorative nature, as is usual in these monuments.

Despite its somewhat prosaic surroundings and the modern iron grating to fend off grazing sheep, this unique and beautifully decorated monolith is one of the great treasures of Celtic La Tène art in Europe. The style of the carving, in its Irish context, is assignable to the last three centuries BC.

The Turoe Stone is a domed granite boulder a little over 3 feet high, artificially shaped and decorated by a technique known as pocking, which sets the design out in relief against the background. The abstract motifs comprise spirals, circles and curves, bounded by a band of simple step pattern carried round the lower part of the stone. The monument was removed to its present site from its place of discovery beside the Rath of Feerwore, an Iron Age ring-fort at Kiltullagh, a few miles away. Its phallic shape can hardly be accidental and it may well represent a fertility cult.

◁ *Dubh Cathair, County Galway* (pp. 88–9)

Dubh Cathair, or Doocaher, 'The Black Fort,' is one of several large stone-built fortifications on Inishmore, Aran. Historically, it has received less attention than famed Dun Aengus, 3½ miles to the north-west, but is scarcely less remarkable a structure and may in fact be considerably older—though none of the Aran forts has been closely dated so far.

The defences at Dubh Cathair consist of a great drystone wall some 200 feet long, curving across the neck of a cliffed limestone promontory which has been spectacularly undercut by the sea. The rampart wall is terraced on three levels on the inside and survives to between 15 and 18 feet in height. Traces of a *chevaux de frise* can be seen outside the fort, while inside are remains of conjoined *clochans*. Like Dun Aengus, the site is exposed to the prevailing westerlies and in its time must have been a comfortless place of habitation, perhaps occupied only intermittently.

There was probably a trivallate hill-fort with concentric earth walls on this elevated site before the large stone cashel, the 'Sun Palace', was built at its centre, perhaps in the fifth or sixth century AD by the ruling O'Neills of Aileach, whose seat it remained until around 1100. Its situation on Greenan Mountain could hardly be bettered, with unrivalled views across the Donegal countryside and the long coastal inlets of Lough Foyle and Swilly. A modern access road to the summit places it within easy reach of the hurried tourist.

The Grianan was extensively reconstructed in the last century from the remains of the cashel wall, which then stood to only 6 feet in height. The fort is now 17 feet high and has a diameter of 77 feet. The wall terraces and connecting stairways may or may not be authentic restorations since little of the original work survived at these levels; but they are representative of the type of construction found in other stone forts of the later Iron Age and Early Christian periods.

The Early Monasteries

THE Irish or Celtic Church grew from the missionary work of several great fifth-century saints of whom Patrick, though not the earliest, was to become the most famous. But the original concept of a church organised on a diocesan principle under the charge of bishops was overwhelmed by the proliferation in the sixth century of semi-independent monasteries controlled by abbots. In the poor and inhospitable lands west of the Shannon, small groups of monks and scholars established anchorite communities in remote locations. The vast number of these remains, fragmentary though many of them are, is a reminder of the vigour with which the monastic spirit swept through Ireland in the Dark Ages. As H.G. Leask has observed, 'there are few habitable islands or suitable coastland sites which do not preserve some relic: some oratory or church, memorial cross or primitive dwelling'.

Though there are substantial remains of ancient churches dotted through the land, nothing now survives of the buildings founded by the missionary saints of the first centuries of Christianity in Ireland. It is from sparse references in the annals, rather than from material evidence in the field, that we are enabled to piece together a fair idea of what the earliest churches looked like. All the accounts point to these having been built mainly of wood, round in shape in the beginning, much in the style of the secular habitations. Later a rectangular plan was adopted. Timber posts and beams hewn from felled trees provided the main framework of the walls and roof, and this was covered with wattles, rushes and mud. Sometimes mud alone was used: it is recorded that St Patrick built an earth-walled church in Co. Mayo because there was a shortage of timber.

It is not known exactly when the first stone churches were built. The transition from timber structures would have been a gradual process influenced to some extent by the nature of local conditions. Along the storm-bound Atlantic seaboard where woodland was scarce and stone plentiful, and where light timber buildings could not in any case be expected to endure, it is probable that building in stone progressed more rapidly; and indeed very many of the oldest surviving stone churches are to be found in western districts. Even so, wood was used whenever it was available, and evidence for timber churches in the west was provided by excavation of a monastic site at Church Island in Valentia harbour, Co. Kerry, where, beneath the foundations of a stone oratory, were found the post-holes of an earlier church built of wood.

The oldest stone churches to survive have architectural features which at once distinguish them from later buildings. They are, as might be expected, of small dimensions, often measuring less than 15 feet long internally, and have a length to width ratio of 1.5:1. They frequently incorporate very large blocks of stone in the lower courses of the walls, and roofs are steeply pitched, imparting a tall, elegant appearance to the building. A fine example of an early stone church is Temple Benen on Inishmore, Co. Galway. The high-pitch of the gables and narrow trabeate (lintelled) doorway with converging jambs are indicative of an early date, possibly in the ninth century.

A feature not found in Temple Benen but common to many ancient churches is the *antae*, a continuation of the side walls beyond the line of the gables, rather like pilaster columns. This non-structural addition is thought to represent the wooden corner posts of timber-built churches, on which their stone-built successors appear to have been modelled. Well preserved antae are to be seen on the little church on St MacDara's Island off the Connemara coast. Here, unusually, they extend all the way up the slope of the gables to the point of the ridge where they are joined by a carved finial. The doorway is characteristically trabeate, the lintel being a massive granite slab some 15 inches thick. The jambs are only moderately splayed, with a width variation of about 2 inches from top to bottom.

Most churches with antae belong to an early period, but this feature is not invariably a mark of antiquity, for antae are found on churches as late as the twelfth century. Equally, some small churches which lack antae are recognised as early structures. Temple Benen is clearly very old, and other islands in the Arans group provide further examples.

While it is probable that the majority of these churches were roofed with thatch or shingles, it is also known that a number had solid stone roofs. Intact stone roofs survive on St Flannan's oratory at Killaloe, Co. Clare, and on St Molaise's oratory on Inishmurray, Co. Sligo (the latter is a nineteenth-century restoration). This kind of roof depended for its durability on the use of mortar, which may not have been widely known in Ireland much before the eighth century. But working in drystone using the corbelling technique of overlapping successive stone courses was practised to considerable effect, enabling small unmortared oratories like Gallarus in the Dingle Peninsula to be built in a way that would endure for a thousand years.

The circular beehive cells, or *clochans*, associated with eremitical sites along the western coasts are also built on the corbelled principle. These diminutive dwellings survive in a well preserved state at spectacular Skellig Michael, appearing today much as they probably did when they were built on this precipitous sea-crag many centuries ago, a testimony to the faith and skill of the small community of religious who lived in total isolation on this Atlantic outpost.

Clochans were not peculiar to monastic settlements, nor are they necessarily early structures; for no other building method has so long or continuous a history in Ireland. Corbelling is found in prehistoric burial monuments and is also a feature of a number of stone ring-forts where it is employed in the construction of wall chambers and souterrains. Comparatively modern clochans are still in use as outbuildings attached to cottage farms in the Dingle Peninsula.

Fundamental to all early monasteries was an encircling earth-work or stone wall within which stood the church and cells of the monks. Most of the earthen banks have been levelled long ago, though their outlines can sometimes be traced when the former existence of a site is known. Stone cashels leave more intelligible remains as a rule, especially if they are located on islands where they are less likely to have been disturbed. If these enclosures remind one of the ring forts of the Celtic chieftains and farmers, the resemblance is more than coincidental. They were, quite simply, adaptations of the secular raths to monastic needs, and there are instances on record of local rulers presenting raths to groups of Christian monks.

An excellent example of an early monastic settlement, complete in many respects, is to be found on Inishmurray, an uninhabited island off the coast of Co. Sligo. The history of Inishmurray is obscure. Seldom mentioned in the annals, it disappears from the records altogether after AD 807 when it was plundered by the Vikings. A similar fate befell scores of vulnerable coastal monasteries in the ninth and tenth centuries. Some like Inishmurray never recovered, but happily the majority appear to have possessed remarkable recuperative powers. Lonely Skellig Michael was raided on several occasions in the first half of the ninth century, but survived to function as 'the most western of Christ's fortresses in the ancient world' for a long time afterwards.

The Viking raids, while often devastating, were not a totally new experience for the Irish monks. Inter-tribal rivalry among powerful Celtic families had been responsible for drawing individual monasteries into bitter and bloody conflict before the Norsemen appeared on the scene, and continued to be a disruptive element after the Viking menace had subsided. But the protracted Viking raids may have been partly responsible for the appearance, around AD 900, of the tall free-standing Round Towers which contribute a distinctly Irish item to the ecclesiastical landscape. These impressive monuments may trace their architectural origins to the humble clochan cells of earlier centuries. But whereas clochans were of drystone construction, Round Towers were built with the aid of mortar, enabling the stone masons to attain heights in excess of 100 feet with total stability. The tapered form of these towers demonstrates the technique of batter: that is, of gradually reducing the thickness of the walls relative to their height, and it is from this characteristic that Round Towers derive their much admired elegance.

It is unlikely that defence was the main reason behind the building of these towers. Their Irish name, *cloigtheach*, means bell-house, and most were probably used as belfries from which hand-bells were rung. But security was clearly taken into account in such matters as the positioning of doorways, which are normally at heights of from 5 to 15 feet above ground level and accessible only by means of a ladder (the only exception is the tower on Scattery Island, Co. Clare, whose doorway is on the ground). In the event of an attack the monks closed themselves inside, taking their monastic treasures with them.

A typical Round Tower has the interior divided into five or six storeys, and though the timber floors of these have disappeared, the various levels can be deduced from the projecting offsets or corbels that carried the beams. Each storey is lighted, rather dimly, by a single window, the topmost by four which gave a lofty all-round view across the surrounding countryside. The top of the tower was finished with a corbelled conical cap rising with a steep pitch from the cornice. It is to be presumed that all Round Towers had this feature, though few remain so complete today. In Medieval times a small number of towers had battlements added for military use. There must at one time have been very many more Round Towers than the present remains of fewer than seventy would suggest, for they continued to be built into the twelfth century.

The magnificent carved crosses which add so much interest

to the monastic scene are in a sense three-dimensional equivalents in stone of the illuminated manuscripts for which the Celtic Church was renowned. Early Christian crosses probably developed from simple outline scribings on pre-existing standing stones, leading to more boldly executed designs in which the cross and its background assume a monumental expressiveness. The great slab at Killaghtee in Co. Donegal, with its confidently cut Maltese cross in a circle, is the work of an accomplished stone-carver. Less formalised but scarcely less striking in its aesthetic effect, is the fine cross-pillar at Reask in Co. Kerry. Later on the stone itself becomes the focus of attention and is carved to an elementary cross shape, like the remarkable series of early crosses on Caher Island, Co. Mayo.

Eventually the fully developed form of the ringed High Cross appears. These stately monuments, richly sculpted with elaborate abstract motifs and figurative panels depicting biblical scenes, represent one of the finest achievements of the artist-craftsmen of the Celtic Church. The beautiful cross at Drumcliff in Co. Sligo, and that at Dysert O'Dea in Co. Clare, are highly developed late examples of the *genre*.

Many of the small nave and chancel churches of early date were not built as such originally. The chancel was as a general rule added to an existing nave, and this kind of extension probably became common in the eleventh century in step with the newer buildings which had a chancel from the outset. Enlargement was achieved by making an arched opening in the east gable wall of the nave and building on the chancel at this point. When this was undertaken in a church with antae, the resulting chancel was of lesser width than the nave; this is clearly seen in the case of Temple MacDuagh on Inishmore, Co. Galway.

By the beginning of the twelfth century, church architecture in Ireland was developing along more sophisticated lines, influenced to a large extent by internal changes taking place in the structure of the monastic system. It was during this period of reorganisation that the Romanesque style, in its unique Irish form, made its appearance. Irish Romanesque is a readily identifiable style, distinguished by round-headed doorways, windows and chancel arches; decorated, sometimes exuberantly, with a rich variety of carved designs based on Celtic, Greek, Roman and Scandinavian motifs. Though not datable with absolute certainty, it is generally accepted that Irish Romanesque belongs to a roughly 100-year period that had its beginnings in the closing years of the eleventh century. Its spread into western districts, where some of the finest work is to be found, was probably more protracted than its assimilation in the east of the country, with the result that the style held sway for longer in the Atlantic coastlands, until it was overtaken by Transitional and Gothic architecture, also slow to penetrate the remoter parts of the west.

A good example of the earlier phase of Irish Romanesque before it had achieved its full-blown form, is St Caimin's church on Iniscealtra, Co. Clare, where the three orders of the chancel arch are plain, decoration being confined to the bases and capitals of the compound piers. The sparing use of ornament indicates a date possibly at the beginning of the twelfth century.

Belonging to a later period than the arch of St Caimin's church and altogether more ambitious in treatment and scale, is the great chancel arch in Tuam cathedral, Co. Galway. Its impressive span of 16 feet exceeds that of any other Irish example. It is decorated on all its six orders, and the cube-like capitals of the supporting columns have interlace designs as well as stylised human heads. Another superb essay in Irish Romanesque is the twelfth-century church at Kilmalkedar in Co. Kerry. But the incomparable achievement of the period is the remarkable west doorway of Clonfert cathedral in Co. Galway. It stands alone, 'the master-work of its class', outstanding both as a piece of stone carving and in the whole concept of its design.

During the first half of the twelfth century, while Irish Romanesque was moving towards its full flowering, far reaching reforms were overtaking the Celtic Church. For a very long time the autonomous monasteries, frequently under lay control, had functioned as independent religious houses, often in fierce competition with one another. Secular motives took precedence and led to much corruption. Earlier attempts at reform, like the Culdee movement of the eighth and ninth centuries, had achieved only temporary local results. Now in the early years of the twelfth century a new religious awareness was gathering momentum in Ireland, stimulated by the tremendous changes taking place in European Christianity. A succession of reforming synods, culminating with the Synod of Kells in 1152, put an end to the disarray of the existing system by imposing a strict diocesan framework on the native church.

Ten years previously, at the instigation of Bishop Malachy of Armagh, the Cistercians of Clairvaux had founded their first Irish house at Mellifont in Co. Louth, designed on the continental plan. Other religious orders soon followed, notably the Augustinians and the Franciscan and Dominican friars. There was, it would seem, no shortage of eager recruits, for the Irish monks quickly deserted their own establishments for the new lifestyle with its emphasis on order and conformity. The old, eclectic world of Celtic monasticism had finally run its course.

◁ *Inishmurray, County Sligo* (p. 99)

This bare and treeless island, often inaccessible because of rough seas and lack of a proper quay, lies 4 miles north-west of Streedagh Point. Charter boat trips leave from Mullaghmore harbour in suitable conditions, the 9-mile crossing taking about 1½ hours. On the island, abandoned by its small beleagured population in the 1950s, are a wealth of remains of the early Christian period. The original monastery was founded in the sixth century by St Molaise and several of the later buildings bear his name. Despite some suspect restoration work carried out in the nineteenth century, mainly on the enclosing wall, the complex provides a substantially authentic picture of the layout of a Celtic monastery. The cashel wall is ovoid in plan, the interior divided into four parts, in the largest of which is Teampull na bFhear, 'the Men's Church,' a pre-Romanesque building with trabeate doorway, and a small stone-roofed church or oratory known as Teach Molaise; it too has a lintelled doorway on which a simple cross is inscribed.

In another sub-enclosure to the north-west is Teampull na Teine, 'Church of the Fire,' also a well preserved drystone *clochan*, formerly inhabited by the monks and more recently utilised as the island schoolhouse. Close by is a *leacht* or altar (one of three) on which lie the much publicised Clocha Breaca ('Speckled Stones'), better known as the Cursing Stones, which can be manipulated to bring down retribution on a wrong-doer. Within the monastery enclosure and distributed round the perimeter of the island are a great number of cross-pillars and slabs, many bearing designs of uncommon beauty.

A place of great and far-reaching fame in Irish ecclesiastical annals, now a popular centre of tourism. Here in the beautiful *Glenn da Locha,* 'Valley of the Two Lakes,' St Kevin established a hermitage in the sixth century. Such was his reputation as a scholar that, contrary to his intention, many came to join him and benefit from his teaching, with the result that a sizeable monastic settlement soon developed. Its expansion in later centuries is evidenced by the remarkable number of monuments distributed through the valley.

The most conspicuous landmark, visible from afar, is the well preserved Round Tower which rises above the tree-tops to a height of 100 feet. Its conical cap was reconstructed in the last century from the original masonry, and the tower can be entered by means of a modern wooden stairway. Nearby St Kevin's Church is a small nave and chancel structure with a stone roof, from which sprouts a belfry in the shape of a miniature Round Tower. Its fancied resemblance to a chimney accounts for the ludicrous name St Kevin's Kitchen by which it has become widely known. Not far away is the Cathedral, a large eleventh and twelfth-century church with sacristy and remnants of a Romanesque chancel arch. There is also some fine Romanesque decoration in St Saviour's Priory, about ¹⁄₂ mile to the east of the main group of buildings.

Altogether the monuments, which include remains of several more churches, a number of stone crosses and ballaun stones, and the monastic gatehouse (the only surviving example in Ireland) extend over a distance of about 1¹⁄₂ miles.

Moone, County Kildare △ (detail, pp. 102–3)

In a walled enclosure outside the village stands this gracile ninth-century High Cross, reassembled from fallen but intact sections found on the site of an early monastery attributed to St Columba. The carving is highly individual, the style outwardly ingenuous yet disarmingly beautiful in its effect. The details remain for the most part crisply defined and the subjects of the various panels can be readily identified, among them the Twelve Apostles, Adam and Eve, the Fiery Furnace, the Flight into Egypt, Miracle of the Loaves and Fishes, and the Crucifixion. There are also representations of mythical beasts.

Beside this cross is the base of another, of interest because the socket on top shows how these free-standing monuments were pieced together. It possibly belongs with the carved fragments preserved in the ruins of a nearby church.

101

◁ ▽ *Kilmalkedar, County Kerry* (*detail*, p. 107)

The ancient monastery of Kilmalkedar, founded in the seventh century by St Maolcathair, is one of the foremost Early Christian sites of the Dingle Peninsula. The existing church is a twelfth-century building consisting of a nave to which a chancel was added at a later date, as was the usual practice. Many of the features which typify Irish Romanesque architecture are present. The bold antae with animal-head decoration are well preserved, as is the round-headed doorway with blank tympanum. The high-pitched gables (one with finial) survive intact, but of the original barrel-vaulted roof only the merest fragments remain. In the nave is a good example of blind colonnading, recalling Cormac's Chapel at Cashel, with which it is often compared. Late-Romanesque geometric motifs adorn the columns of the chancel arch.

A number of interesting objects stand outside the church. These include a tall slender Ogham stone perforated with a circular hole near the top; a large ringless cross devoid of any decoration and therefore possibly unfinished; and a beautiful sundial stone marked in segments corresponding to the divisions of the monastic day.

Most isolated and spectacular of all Irish monastic sites, this dark oceanic crag rises precipitously out of the Atlantic 8 miles west of Bolus Head. Huddled on a wind-swept rock plateau nearly 600 feet above the sea is a small group of ancient buildings, lonely relics of an anchorite monastery founded by St Finan and dedicated, appropriately, to St Michael, patron saint of high places.

The monastery is contained by a well preserved drystone wall and is reached by a succession of stone steps leading steeply upwards from three landing places round the island, their use dictated by weather conditions. Today's visitors ascend by the more intact southern stairway which connects with the cliff road to the lighthouse, engineered by George Halpin in 1820. The remains comprise six beehive cells or *clochans*, two small oratories and a ruined medieval church. There are also a number of cross-pillars and slabs, some of which line the edge of a little raised plot of man-made land known as 'the Monks' Garden.' Historical records for the monastery are scant, but it is recorded that it was attacked by the Vikings on at least four occasions during the first half of the ninth century. The settlement may have been abandoned at the end of the twelfth century when it seems the monks moved to Ballinskelligs on the Kerry mainland.

Access to Skellig is at best uncertain and landing on the rock is possible only in calm sea conditions. In suitable weather in summer, boat trips depart from Derrynane and Cahirciveen, and from Knightstown or Valentia Island.

◁ *Gallarus, County Kerry*

A remarkably well preserved drystone
oratory built on the corbelled principle.
Its shape, often likened to an upturned
boat, is unusual though not unique in
early Irish churches, and several ruined
examples of the type are known in this
part of Kerry. It has the typically lintelled
doorway of pre-Romanesque churches,
with markedly converging jambs, and
measures 15 feet by 10 feet internally; this
length to breadth ratio is also indicative
of churches built before the twelfth
century. A tiny round-headed window is
set in the east gable wall. Despite its
evident antiquity (though it is not
necessarily to be placed among the earliest
stone churches), the skilfully laid stone
courses remain thoroughly watertight.

Of the monastery of Drumcliff, said to have been founded by St Columcille in the sixth century, only the elaborately sculptured High Cross and the base of a Round Tower survive. The former dates possibly from the early years of the eleventh century and is decorated on both faces with scriptural scenes, interlace designs and zoomorphic motifs. Among the biblical episodes depicted are the Crucifixion, Adam and Eve, and Daniel in the Lions' Den.

Close by is Drumcliff Parish Church, in the graveyard of which, 'Under bare Ben Bulbin's Head,' the poet W.B. Yeats is buried.

(detail)

Arboe, County Tyrone ▷

This well known monument stands at
Arboe Point, 'the Hill of the Cow,' on the
west shore of Lough Neagh. It is a
particularly fine specimen and belongs to
a late period in the development of the
sculptured free-standing ringed crosses. In
its present form it is a reconstruction, the
upper part having fallen in 1846, and now
stands 18 feet high. The carved details
depict biblical scenes some of which are
self evident—Miracle of the Loaves and
Fishes, the Crucifixion, David and
Goliath, the Last Supper, Cain and Abel,
etc.—but weathering has obscured the
meaning of other panels. There was a
monastery hereabouts in the sixth century
and pilgrimages were until fairly recently
made to the site.

114

The oldest surviving artefacts of the Celtic church are the cross-pillars and slabs found at a number of monastic sites throughout the country. They represent the first tentative steps in the development of Irish ecclesiastical art. Unlike the later ringed crosses which evolved from them, the earliest Christian crosses were simply inscribed on suitable natural stones with no attempt at shaping. Sometimes *in situ* pagan standing stones were adopted for the purpose.

The Reask cross-pillar is one of several early monuments recently discovered at an ancient enclosure in the west of the Dingle peninsula. It is among the most exquisite of its type and in the few years since it came to light it has attracted widespread attention. The late influence of Celtic La Tène decoration is implicit in the flowing spiral patterns, while the incorporation of the bold intrinsic facets of the stone into the overall design is especially striking, producing a harmony of line and form that is aesthetically very pleasing. The abbreviated inscription *dne* running vertically down the side of the stone is presumably dedicatory.

Two small additional cross-pillars have lately been uncovered and erected alongside; on one of these is an unusual bird motif. Other remains here include the bases of conjoined clochans, the ruins of a small oratory and part of the monastery wall. Results of excavation indicate that the site was in use over a long period.

Dalkey Island, County Dublin (p. 118) ▷

A small treeless island 300 yards offshore from Coliemore harbour, where row-boats may be hired. The island is uninhabited and its main interest is the early church dedicated to St Begnet near the landing place on the west shore. It has prominent *antae* and a massively lintelled doorway with slightly inclined jambs. The original roof was probably thatch or shingles, but medieval slates discovered in the course of excavation show that the church remained in use for some considerable time. The bell cote on the west gable is also a late addition. Alterations were made to the interior of the building at the beginning of the nineteenth century when it was temporarily occupied by the workmen who constructed the Martello tower on the island.

On a weathered rock outside the church is an inscribed cross in a circle, a relic perhaps of the first monastery here, possibly in the sixth or seventh century. Of the founder, St Begnet, nothing is known.

△ Temple Benen, County Galway

A diminutive early church or oratory, prominently situated on a bare limestone ridge above the village of Killeany on Inishmore, largest of the three Aran Islands in Galway bay. It takes its name from a fifth-century saint, Benen or Benignus, but is later than his time. It is however of considerable antiquity and several of its features are indicative of a date possibly in the eight or ninth century: the steeply pitched gables, narrow trabeate doorway with inclined jambs, and the exceptional size of the stones in the side walls. The interior is only 7 feet wide.

There are traces of clochans and other monastic remains in the vicinity, including the base of a Round Tower which collapsed in the nineteenth century.

A twelfth-century cathedral (St Brendan's) with thirteenth-century extensions. Despoiled in the sixteenth century, it was clumsily restored at various times afterwards and now serves as the Protestant parish church of Clonfert. The carved decoration, inside and out, is of exceptional quality, and the great west doorway ranks as the masterwork of Irish Romanesque art. Built in warm-toned sandstone, it is composed of six orders (the seventh, innermost order in limestone is a fifteenth-century insertion) and is notable for the exaggerated splay of the jambs. The variety of ornamental devices is remarkable, an eclectic inventory of the stone mason's repertoire comprising geometric designs, human and animal heads, interlace patterns and foliage. Above the arch is a pediment-like hood, the gable of which is filled with carved heads set in triangular niches and supported on a panel of blind arcading. Many of the motifs and architectural features are rare in Irish Romanesque and some are unique to Clonfert.

Glencolumbkille, County Donegal (p. 122) ▷

There are many venerated relics of the past, both prehistoric and early Christian, in this rugged coastal valley inseparably linked with the name of St Columcille, or Columba. The most interesting survivals are the great number of cross-slabs and pillars distributed over a wide area and which now, together with several pre-Christian megalithic monuments, form the stations of a pilgrim 'pattern' held annually on 9 June. The complete circuit of the incorporated monuments covers a distance of some 3 miles. One of the finest of the cross-pillars stands on a rocky knoll by the roadside 100 yards south of the Protestant churchyard, where the pilgrimage begins and ends. It is decorated with key motifs of a type rare in Ireland. Another pillar to the north of the church is pierced with a circular hole through which, it is said, the penitent is afforded a view of heaven.

◁ *Monasterboice, County Louth* (p. 123)

Though little more than half a mile to the west of the busy Dublin road, there is an air of detachment and antiquity about this celebrated place. The monastery came into existence in the sixth century but little is known of its founder, St Buite. Its fame rests chiefly on its exquisitely sculptured High Crosses, notably the South Cross, now generally called Muiredach's Cross after an abbot whose name is inscribed on the base. The cross is remarkable for the variety and organisation of its scriptural themes and the superb quality of the carving, executed in the early decades of the tenth century.

Not far away, beside the Round Tower (now capless but still over 90 feet high), is the slender and beautiful West Cross, *alias* the Tall Cross, from its exceptional height of 21 feet. It has suffered from weathering and not all of its panels are identifiable. In another corner of the graveyard, partly obscured by trees and sometimes missed by visitors, is the North Cross. Though not as elaborate as the other two it is nevertheless a fine specimen, decorated with unusual spiral motifs. A handsome sundial stone stands alongside. Other remains here include two featureless churches.

Dysert O Dea, County Clare (p. 126) ▷

St Tola founded a monastery here in the seventh or eighth century. The present church on the site is a late Medieval reconstruction of an earlier, Romanesque building whose magnificent west doorway is incorporated in the south wall. The finely carved motifs of the arch include geometric designs and unusual human masks. Close behind the north wall of the church is a shattered Round Tower built in the twelfth century.

On rising ground not far to the east of the church is an interesting High Cross. It also dates from the twelfth century and comes right at the end of the Celtic High Cross series. It is of the ringless type found elsewhere in Co. Clare, and is elaborately decorated with interlace and geometric designs, as well as figurative panels in high relief. An inscription on the base records that it was repaired in 1683 by a member of the O Dea family.

Bibliography

Archaeological Survey of Northern Ireland: County Down Belfast, H.M.S.O., 1966

Barber, J. 'The Orientation of the Recumbent-stone Circles of the South-West of Ireland' *Journal of the Kerry Archaeological and Historical Society* 1973, vol. 6, no. 26

Borlase, W.C. *Dolmens of Ireland* 3 vols., London, 1897

Burl, A. *The Stone Circles of the British Isles* Yale, 1976

Craig, M., and Glin, Knight of *Ireland Observed* Cork, 1970

Davies, O. 'Stone Circles in Northern Ireland' *Ulster Journal of Archaeology* 1939, vol. 2, no. 2

de Breffny, B. and Mott, G. *In the steps of St Patrick* London, 1982

de Valera, R. and O Nuallain, S. *Survey of the Megalithic Tombs of Ireland* 4 vols., Dublin 1. Co. Clare, 1961; II. Co. Mayo, 1964; III. the Counties of Galway, Roscommon, Leitrim, Cavan, Longford and Westmeath, 1967; IV. the Counties of Cork and Kerry, in preparation

Dunraven, Lord *Notes on Irish Architecture* London, 1875

Evans, E.E. *Prehistoric and Early Christian Ireland* London, 1966

Fergusson, J. *Rude Stone Monuments* London, 1872

Gray, W. 'The Cromlechs of Antrim and Down' *Proceedings of the Belfast Naturalists' Field Club* 1883-4, Appendix, p.225

Harbison, P. *The Archaeology of Ireland* London, 1976
Ireland Before St Patrick Dublin, 1978
Guide to the National Monuments of Ireland Dublin, 1979

Henry, F. *Irish Art in the Early Christian Period* London, 1965
Irish Art in the Romanesque Period London, 1970

Herity, M. *Glencolumkille* Dublin, 1971
Irish Passage Graves Dublin, 1975

Herity, M. and Eogan, G. *Ireland in Prehistory* London, 1977

Hickey, H. *Images of Stone* Belfast, 1976

Historic Monuments of Northern Ireland Hamlin, A. (ed.), Belfast, H.M.S.O., 1983

Killanin, Lord, and Duignan, M. V. *Shell Guide to Ireland* London, 1969

Leask, H.G. *Irish Churches and Monastic buildings* Dundalk, 1955
'The Long Stone, Punchestown, Co. Kildare' *Journal of the Royal Society of Antiquaries of Ireland* 1937, vol. 67, no. 250

Macalister, R.A.S. *Ireland in Pre-Celtic Times* London, 1921

Movius, H.J. *The Irish Stone Age* London, 1942

O Nuaillain, S. 'The Stone Circle Complex of Cork and Kerry' *Journal of the Royal Society of Antiquaries of Ireland* 1975, vol. 105, no. 83

O Riordain, S.P. *Antiquities of the Irish Countryside* London, 1979

Pochin Mould, D.D.C. *The Monasteries of Ireland* London, 1976

Preliminary Survey of the Ancient Monuments of Northern Ireland Chart, D.A. (ed.), Belfast, H.M.S.O., 1940

Raftery, J. *Prehistoric Ireland* London, 1951

Somerville, B.T. 'Ancient Stone Monuments near Lough Swilly, County Donegal' *Journal of the Royal Society of Antiquaries of Ireland* 1929, vol. 59, no. 149

'Five Stone Circles of West Cork' *Journal of the Cork Historical and Archaeological Society* 1930, vol. 35, no. 70

Weir, A. *Early Ireland: a Field Guide* Belfast, 1980

Westropp, T. J. 'The Ancient forts of Ireland' *Transactions of the Royal Irish Academy* 1896-1901, Dublin, vol. 31, no. 579
'The Promontory Forts and Early Remains of the Islands of Connacht' *Journal of the Royal Society of Antiquaries of Ireland* Dublin, 1914, vol. XLIV, no. 297

Wood-Martin, W.G. *The Rude Stone Monuments of Ireland* Dublin, 1888
Pagan Ireland London, 1895
Traces of the Elder Faiths of Ireland 2 vols. London, 1902